BRITAIN IN OLD PHOTOGRAPHS

LANCASHIRE

CATHERINE ROTHWELL

SUTTON PUBLISHING

Sutton Publishing Limited
Phoenix Mill · Thrupp · Stroud
Gloucestershire · GL5 2BU

First published 1996

Copyright © Catherine Rothwell, 1996

British Library Cataloguing in Publication Data
A catalogue record for this book is available from the
British Library.

ISBN 0-7509-1302-9

Typeset in 10/12 Perpetua.
Typesetting and origination by
Sutton Publishing Limited.
Printed in Great Britain by
Ebenezer Baylis, Worcester.

CONTENTS

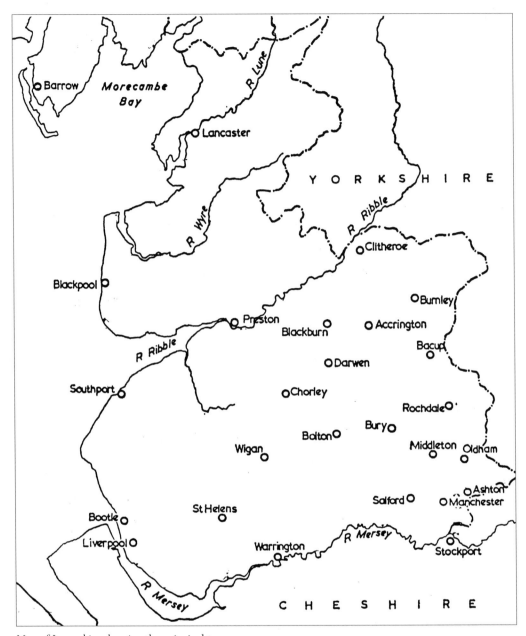

Map of Lancashire showing the principal towns.

INTRODUCTION

Lancashire is a county of great contrast, and much of what was in the old palatinate has vanished. The growth of industry, the sprawl of urbanism and the boundary changes of 1974 have led to some of the most beautiful scenery in all England, once in Lancashire, being lost to the shire. With over 270 photographs, this book aims to recapture the old county of Lancaster so that we can compare and contrast old with new. The newness is currently expressed in high streets as alike as peas in a pod, screaming high-tech wares and household names. Shopping malls have brought anonymity. One may wonder, 'Which town are we in?' With the passing of old trades and crafts, customs and street signs went the character that had stamped an unforgettable uniqueness on both places and minds. Imagine: '43 blacksmiths and 6 bird and animal dealers and preservers' in one Lancashire town alone; a Preston boot and shoe shop carried the sign of a large, golden boot above its portals; and Caffin's Eye-glasses mounted a pair of gilded spectacles across the frontage of its premises in Fishergate.

In the nineteenth century and well into the twentieth, 'King Cotton' ruled over such countless acres (indeed occupied whole towns) that his legacy could not be completely erased. Dunlop Cotton Mills, built by Oldham architect Sydney Stott in 1914 (the final extension being completed in 1927), was the largest cotton mill in the world under one roof. Tonge Moor Textile Museum in Bolton and Lewis Textile Museum in Blackburn, once thriving mills, exist mutely today as showpieces of an industry that influenced the globe. Platt Brothers in 1881 was the largest machine-making firm in Europe, at a time when Oldham produced seven newspapers and Wigan raised 7 million tons of coal yearly. It is certain that Lancashire made an unparalleled contribution to Great Britain's economic growth in the nineteenth century.

In this forcing atmosphere, fortunes were made and pioneers were bred. Fierce competition led to Lancashire becoming a county of 'firsts', in railways, libraries, canals, free trade, the Co-operative Movement, the Temperance Movement and public offices of health. Bury, Blackburn, Bolton and Preston produced inventors to pace ever faster that giant, the Industrial Revolution. The production of textiles alone was transformed by John Kay, James Hargreaves, Richard Arkwright and Samuel Crompton. In poor Samuel's case he received only £60 while mill owners became millionaires, with 11.5 million spindles in one factory. Warrington ladies worked for 2d. a day making sail cloth. The cities of Liverpool and Manchester, industrial centres of the county, both received their Charters of Incorporation in 1832 and were connected by the country's first railway. Liverpool claimed to be the second city in the empire, and certainly the world's biggest ships belonged to Liverpool. Later they joined in the amazing Victorian achievement of linking the inland city with the sea by means of the Ship Canal.

Yet amid the burgeoning smoke and turmoil of intensive industry, art galleries and orchestras to rival those of London were forming. Poets and writers chronicled the sweat and agony of workers in mines and mills. Philanthropists too came forward to ease pain and promote education: Elizabeth Gaskell, Thomas Henshaw and John Rylands. In this county, rich in people and places, famous names abound: Kathleen Ferrier, Isobel Baillie, Celia Fiennes, Robert Gillow, Samuel Horrocks and W.P. Hartley. E.H. Booth was a pauper boy who rose to become the founder of a grocery chain established in 1847 and still going strong. The unrivalled pioneering spirit had bred a desire for excellence and there was enough 'brass' to achieve it. 'Manchester is the most musically civilized city in the world,' Sir John Barbirolli, conductor of the Hallé Orchestra, was to say. The first concerts commenced in 1744, and alongside musical tradition grew the choral societies, massed choirs, massed bands and massed processions. Big was an expression of beautiful; or was it of power? Lancastrians worked hard and played hard. Out of this thrust grew Blackpool, the most popular seaside resort in the world and the one with the greatest flair, attracting, of course, world-class performers and setting up its own record for 'firsts'.

The universities of Manchester, Liverpool, Lancaster and now that of Central Lancashire, UMIST, and the technical colleges, were all cradled in an atmosphere of energetic desire to seek and find. In its day Dr John Seddon's Warrington Academy was a model for the world, carried forward by such brilliant scholars as chemist Joseph Priestley.

The city fathers who poured from such bursting cornucopias had great ideas. Rochdale's town hall, which was built between 1861 and 1871 and designed by Crossland of Leeds, was in grand metropolitan style. Its exchange within had a carved staircase and sixteen angels supporting the hammer-beam roof. Portaits of kings and queens lined the Great Hall together with Henry Halliday's fresco, an artist numbered among William Morris and his Pre-Raphaelites. Near the town hall was placed the great Thorneycroft bronze statue of Rochdale's most famous citizen, John Bright. It was in Rochdale where Edwin Waugh, 'The Lancashire Burns', was born, not to mention that great-hearted lady with the golden voice, Gracie Fields, who loved Blackpool but went to live on Capri.

It is almost 650 years since Lancashire became a county palatinate. Since the days of Henry IV, the son of 'Old John of Gaunt, time-honoured Lancaster', the dukedom has been held by the reigning monarch and the county's proud toast is 'The Queen, Duke of Lancaster!' The town's castle is glorious but grim, for assizes held there since 1176 are said to have sentenced to death more people than in any crown court in the country: 'Isaac Slater, for stealing printed calico, along with 7 others associated with crimes ranging from highway robbery to forgery, was executed on September 12th 1820.' Such occasions were enjoyed by the populace and regarded as a holiday.

Even an exhaustive gazetteer of Lancashire could not mention all places, yet one might argue that the smallest hamlet is as important as the greatest city if it contains a pearl of great price. Those secret valleys to which the Quakers fled for refuge 'in the wilds of Lancashire', tucked-away courtyards, the fuller's field by the river, a stretch of petrified forest, a boat-builder's yard, chains and solitary anchor dripping red rust, a nettle-grown field – site of a Bronze Age settlement – the constantly shifting sand dunes that from time to time reveal ships wrecked a hundred years ago, even a tiny chapel on what was once the edge of the sea – all are part of the old Lancashire that to explore and study is to be rewarded.

May this collection of photographs expressing the manners and ways of many yesterdays provoke memory and give zest to the swiftly passing years.

GREAT CITIES AND THEIR SATELLITES

Owen's College, Manchester, 1910.

The New Royal Infirmary, Manchester, 1927. The infirmary was opened by HRH Princess Mary, Viscountess Lascelles, and a souvenir brochure was issued to mark the occasion.

Princess Mary, later designated Princess Royal, daughter of King George V and Queen Mary. Like her great-grandmother Queen Victoria, she was concerned about hospitals and nursing. On the occasion of the visit of Queen Victoria on 10 October 1851, the inmates of the old infirmary 'made merry, assisted by sticks arm-slings and crutches'. They spread out along the 615 ft length of the infirmary pond. Three large fountains between Mosley Street and Portland Street delighted Her Majesty. On the previous day at Patricroft, 'rain-poikels', as the unremitting rain of Manchester was then known, marred the passage of state barges and the decorated regatta boats, but did not prevent 70,000 Manchester children from lustily singing the National Anthem.

PICCADILLY, MANCHESTER

Piccadilly, Manchester, *c.* 1917. This popular area, once known as 'Piccadilly Flags', was proverbial for military parades, guards of honour, political speeches and as a general meeting place for friends and relatives. On May Day, 1824, the Rush Cart was dragged through, as it had been in previous years when the old tradition of strewing rushes on the church floor still took place. Many members of parliament began their careers as orators in Piccadilly. A 1796 handbill referred to a race held here: 'At the Circus, November 2nd 1796. A foot-race by Mr Wild ('Stump') and another noted runner for 10 guineas, twelve times round, making 800 yards.' A unique private library was housed in Piccadilly in 1874, specializing in 'anything scarce or peculiar especially in local literature'. There was a well-known literary coterie in this area, that included James Crossley of Cavendish Place who practised law in Manchester until 1860. It was he who started the library. An ardent collector of books and a frequent contributor to *Blackwood's Magazine*, he presided at the Philobiblion Society and was president of the Cheltenham Society. It is interesting to note that Mr John Wild, famous at the Kersal Moor Races, was still running at the age of 80. He was a native of Laneside near Milnrow where the public house sign painted in his honour read: 'Stump and Pie Lad'.

The Shambles, Manchester, 1904. Wine and spirit merchant Samuel Kelly stands beside the five barrels outside the Dragon Inn. On the left was a restaurant and Chambers the hairdresser, while on the right was Market Place.

The London, Midland and Scottish Railway locomotive *Amethyst* No. 45700 heads a passenger train about to leave Manchester Victoria Station for Carlisle on 16 May 1962. At that time, through services ran from Manchester Victoria to Glasgow, and to Heysham to connect with the Belfast boat.

The Royal Exchange, Manchester, 1935. This fine building expresses the commercial rise of the City of Manchester. In the 1940s it was burned by German incendiary bombs at the same time as the Free Trade Hall suffered the same fate. The first Exchange, of classical design, was built in Market Place in 1729 and taken down in 1792, the building materials being bought by a Mr Upton of Church Street. An old resident claimed in 1874 that he had seen in Mr Upton's yard at Bank Top the two spikes, still fastened to the stones, on which the heads of the Jacobite rebels Dean and Syddall had been impaled. At the dying wish of 90-year-old Miss Hale of King Street the heads were buried in the consecrated ground of St Ann's Church. At the time of the rebellion, Prince Charles Edward had slept in Mr Dickenson's fine house in Market Street Lane. By 1809 a larger building was needed, and again more space was required in 1845. To accommodate the increasing number of firms and subscribers connected with the cotton trade in the 1870s, the 'Royal' was rebuilt yet again. Membership had reached 12,000 and, twice a week, buying and selling was conducted in the Great Hall. At its peak, the Royal Exchange was internationally famous. However, between the First and Second World Wars, trade declined. Now the Great Hall accommodates the Exchange Theatre. Crisis in the cotton market, 1952 was caused by foreign import restrictions. The Argentine, South African and Australian markets were lost, putting 60,000 people out of work.

Manchester United, FA Cup Winners 1909. Back row, left to right: Ernest Mangnall (manager), Fred Bacon (trainer), Jack Picken, ? Edmonds, Mr McMurray (director), Harry Moger, John H. Davies (chairman), T. Hower, Mr G. Lawton, Alex Bell and Mr Deakin. Middle row: Billy Meredith, Dick Duckworth, Charlie 'the ghost' Roberts, Sandy Turnbull, Enoch West, -?-. Those seated in the front row are not known.

The Great Northern Railway Company's goods warehouse, Salford, early 1970s. At this time the building was empty and derelict, and the yard had become an NCP car park. Old notices about Central Station still lingered. English Heritage has placed restrictions on the reuse of this building, an interesting pile for the industrial archaeologist.

Old houses facing the Bull's Head, Greengate, Salford, 1898. These buildings were demolished in 1901. The overhanging upper storey indicates buildings of great age. Although the notice on the lamp (far right) reads 'Flying Dutchman Inn', this public house was no longer in business. Greengate once guarded Salford's pastureland but the Industrial Revolution changed that. The Greengate Rubber and Leather Works, which was owned by Isidor Frankenburg and was founded in 1867 with only twelve staff, experienced a phenomenal rise to success. It is not easy to think of Salford as a spa, but in the eighteenth century there was reference to 'an ancient cold bath called The Spaw, well known for its plentiful supply of spring water'. In 1796, when filled up for public use at 6d. a time, towels were included. Although industrial premises crowded the baths out, Spaw Street lived on. At the foot of Greenbank was Paradise Vale near Broughton Bridge. The River Irwell frequently overflowed on to the lush meadows. Nearby there was a common where children fished in the ponds. Springfield Lane, later densely packed with dwellings, was then fringed with sweet-smelling hawthorn. By 1874, Wheat Hill 'had not an ear of corn to bless it', Richard Wright Procter, *Memorials of Manchester Streets*, 1874; neither was there fruit or flowers in Spring Field, Garden Lane, Blossoms Street or Old Orchard.

Salford Docks on the Manchester Ship Canal, 1908. Mill chimneys and warehouses are much in evidence. When the Corn Laws were repealed in 1846, Manchester and Salford celebrated together in a procession of brass bands, Lord Mayors from all over Lancashire, lodges, fire brigades and lamplighters, Free Trade bringing wealth to both cities.

Chapel Street, Salford, 1899. By the lamp was the Old Ship Inn, Wine and Spirit Merchants, owned by F. Leech. The *Daily News* shop, outside which a bystander reads despatches of the Boer War, sells *Lloyds News*. Whitworth's *Manchester Magazine* and the *Mercury* would also have been available.

Poster advertising the Co-operative Wholesale Society Ltd. The society had a wood box and crate works in Vere Street, Salford, their milk bottles being made at Worksop and Pendleton. The horsedrawn cart was used when the daily milk round was inaugurated in the 1900s, but it was eventually replaced by electric vehicles. Some streets were named after Salford people. Broster Street near Broughton Bridge derived from a benefactor, Charles Broster, who left £100 for coal and clothing for the poor. He was buried in Manchester Cathedral. Sarah Brearcliffe, also a philanthropist, was remembered by Brearcliffes Buildings, Gravel Lane. She bequeathed £3,000 in 1803 to '14 decayed housekeepers of Manchester and Salford'. 'Old Grindrod', consisting of two meadows, was so called because John Grindrod died on the gibbet there.

Swinton tram No. 56, early 1900s. This tram travelled via New Bentley Street and Pendleton. Manchester's trams had run since 1901. The last one, bound for the depot, was watched by a small group as it turned into Slade Lane from Stockport Road on 10 January 1949.

The Bull's Head Inn, Greengate, Salford, 1907. This was a well-known hostelry. The Seven Stars Inn, Manchester, was 'the oldest licensed house in Great Britain, licensed over 540 years' and operating at the same time as the Bull's Head.

Worsley village, 1910. The church tower and spire are situated amid lime trees not far from the nineteenth-century Worsley Hall and Court House. A Jacobean armchair and a 300-year-old pulpit are among the church's treasures.

Great Jackson Street corner near City Road, Hulme, 1939. Tram lines, setts and shop signs betray the customs and habits of sixty years ago as do the motorcycles, the sale of coke fuel notice and a shop (right) devoted to pipes, tobacco and cigarettes.

The Co-operative Wholesale Society's Soap Works, Irlam, c. 1930. Since its inception at Rochdale, the Movement had grown greatly with custom-built factories producing commodities for its branches. There was a large biscuit works at Crumpsall that produced 3 tons of biscuits a day. The society's tobacco factory was established in 1898 at Angel Meadow, Salford.

Talbot Road, Old Trafford, *c.* 1895. The Manchester Carriage and Tramways Company provided this horsedrawn tram for the use of Old Trafford All Saints' Infirmary. It stands waiting at Trafford Bar.

Seymour Park School, Old Trafford. During the Second World War this school served as No. 2 First Aid Post. Two nurses practise stretcher drill amid sandbagged buildings. The townspeople arranged rotas for firewatching, every night being covered, with heightened alert at full moon.

Westinghouse Tower, Trafford Park, 1920s. This area became intensely busy as a result of the arrival of the Manchester Ship Canal. Extensive railway systems existed at both Manchester and Liverpool docks. Construction of the East Lancashire Road in the 1920s and the opening of the Mersey Tunnel in 1934 brought Liverpool and Manchester closer, and with an intricate network of canals Trafford Park became the hub of communication vital to the ports' trade. A century before the arrival of warehouses, plus chemical and engineering firms, Trafford Hall, in splendid isolation, was kept by a Miss Ryle.

Trafford Road, Trafford Park, 1905. 'Wake up England, Trafford Park is awake' emblazoned the decorative arch welcoming King Edward VII when he opened No. 9 dock of the Manchester Ship Canal.

The Empire Theatre, Ardwick, early 1900s. 'A very nice theatre inside and they do get some good turns here. Mark Sheridan, one of the B boys, tops the bill', wrote Hannah to Jack on the back of this postcard.

Barton Aqueduct, Manchester Ship Canal, 1906. The Duke of Bridgewater's canal crossed the River Irwell here by means of a large, stone, three-arched aqueduct built by engineer James Brindley. Daniel Adamson's project for Manchester made the city the fourth port in Great Britain. An American engineer judged it the most efficient in Europe.

'Top of Hope', Pendleton, 1905. At regular intervals the Pendleton Fault, exacerbated by coal-mining, used to shift, causing alarming minor earthquakes. Subsidence led to houses sinking and, in 1954, two in Temple Drive, Swinton, disappeared completely into Black Harry Tunnel.

Higher Openshaw, 1916. The walk to Gorton Reservoir was a favourite with families at the end of the working week. Behind the reservoir was a park, thronged on fine Sundays and Easter Monday.

The Alhambra Theatre, Openshaw, 1916. This was typical of theatres in the Manchester area. The Alhambra Pavilion, adjoining, showed 'pictures, twice nightly at 7 and 9, with matinees on Monday, Thursday and Saturday'.

Hugh Mason's Monument, Ashton-under-Lyne, c. 1920. During a religious riot in 1868, courageous Hugh, a cotton magnate, read the Riot Act and tried to control the crowd. In June 1917 a munitions factory blew up in Ashton, killing forty-seven people.

F.S. Sowersby's pastrycook and confectioner's shop, *c.* 1912. This was part of old Urmston. Above the shop was a restaurant where luncheons, dinners and teas were served daily. Mr Sowersby was also a wine merchant to whom customers could bring their own tankard or bottle to be filled. 'Direct from the barrel to the consumer' was his proud boast. Port, sherry, claret, beef and malt wine, and white port were available in a 'large, dock glass' at prices ranging from 4d. to 8d.

Flixton Road, 1930. At this time Douglas Fairbanks was appearing in *Mr Robinson Crusoe* at the Palace, as seen on the advertisement to the right. Ambleside Road is on the right and Flixton Station Bridge is nearby. Flixton had an old-fashioned cobbler's shop and a regular 'Stop me and buy one' tricycle ice-cream man.

Manchester Road, Chorlton-cum-Hardy, 1913. Note the two trams, a traditional streetlamp and well-protected young trees in a growing Manchester suburb. Tram services into and out of the city were excellent.

Westminster Road School, Droylsden, c. 1920. 'Standard Two, the Girls' Department' reveals a well-ordered classroom bright with flowers and forty-five little girls.

J.C. Kidd's chemist's shop, 551 Cheetham Hill Road, 1920. 'Teeth carefully extracted' indicates that Mr Kidd was also the local dentist. The huge, glass Winchesters filled with coloured liquid were in those days the recognized signs of a chemist's shop. Similarly, a red-and-white striped pole indicated a barber's shop.

Cheetham Hill village, c. 1900. The splendid street furniture includes a cast-iron octagonal pillar box, lamp standards and a No. 157 open-topped tram. A large Jewish community of excellent tailors grew up here because of the proximity of the village to Manchester.

Sedgley Park wedding, August 1940. Cpl Herbert Bailey of the Pay Corps married Miss Nora Green, whose bridesmaids were inseparable school friends all aged 20, dressed in lace and chiffon as these materials required no clothing coupons. At the far left is Alan Green, the best man, Joan Mitchell, Herbert Bailey, Nora Green, Edna Smith, Catherine Houghton.

Heaton Park rustic bridge, 1902. Purchased by Manchester Corporation from the Earl of Wilton, the Heaton Park estate had woods, streams, rose gardens, a lake and a temple observatory set on a hill from where Royton's mill chimney, one of the tallest in Lancashire, could be seen. The park's greatest glory was Heaton Hall Museum and Art Gallery, which was open to the public.

Prestwich Clough, 1920s. Part of the Irwell Valley, this was a place of rustic bridges, streams and trees. On the hill stands the fifteenth-century church of St Mary, in the churchyard of which is buried William Sturgeon, a pioneer of electricity.

Miss Edna Smith, 16 July 1938. Edna, of Heaton Park Methodist Church, was chosen as Rose Queen elect for the Grand Carnival at Prestwich. Local churches took turns for the privilege. The annual carnival featured brass bands, Morris dancers, motor floats, horsedrawn tableaux, mounted police, and landaus carrying the Rose Queen, her retinue and leading civic dignitaries. That year the carnival was in aid of the building fund for Grimshaw's Playing Fields on Heys Road. The official handbook of twenty-five pages and with a bright orange cover cost just 3d.

Besses o' th' Barn Brass Band, 1906. That year the band went on tour from Windsor to France. Famous for its brass and silver bands, Lancashire had one of the best known at Besses near Whitefield. It won many trophies and attended the opening of Fleetwood Dock in 1877.

The Croft Laundry Company Ltd, Whitefield, 1930s. This company was very busy at this time because if offered an excellent service. Socks and stockings were darned and shirt buttons renewed free of charge. A blanket could be washed for only 5d. and blown dry outside. Not far away was Hall's Toffee Works, which smelled delicious to scholars of Stand Grammar School as they entrained at Whitefield Station. The school, founded in 1688, was supposedly attended by Robert Clive of India when as a boy he lived at Clifton Hall. It is said that to get to school he forded the River Irwell on horseback.

Long Street, Middleton, 1930s. The New Inn is on the right. Duckworth Ltd had taken over the ground floor of the 1895 building (left) on Manchester Old Road. Middleton was once well known for its clock-making trade.

The old cotton mill, Park Bridge, on the main Oldham to Ashton road, 1900. Park Bridge was a complete industrial hamlet with mills, cottages, the owner's house, canal and horsedrawn trams. Powered by the River Medlock, the mill was owned by Samuel and Hannah Lees in the nineteenth century.

Mr Eric Wardle, butcher, at the door of his shop in Inkerman Street, Oldham, *c.* 1910. A hundred years before, this area was known as 'Bottom o't Moor'. In 1881 there were 303 cotton spinning mills in Oldham making fustians, velveteens and corduroys.

The High Street, Oldham, 1901. Blind Joe, the bellman, cried the news up and down Oldham's streets for forty years. In appreciation, a statue of top-hatted Joseph Howarth with his familiar bell and stick was placed in Alexandra Park. Oldham and Bolton were considered the greatest spinning towns, with Blackburn and Burnley the big weaving towns.

Shaw Cycling Club, 1890. This intrepid group dates from the days of velocipedes and dandy chargers. Left to right: J. Cooling, T. Taylor, J.W. Cockcroft, E. Fielding, R. Hanson, J. Pritchard, J. Whitehead, B. Sugden (captain), J. Butterworth, G. Cooling, S. Whitehead, G. Steele and C.H. Riley. A good testing ground for new 'iron steeds' was over the new bridge into Strangeways, Manchester.

Coronation celebrations, Stanley Street Mill, Chadderton, 1911. Left to right: Mary Green, Lizzie Makinson, Clara Richmond, Bessie Naylor and Cissie Dean.

Oldham Corporation tram No. 4, a four-wheeled balcony car, 1920. As this tram climbs to the Market Place an open-topped model travels towards Hollinwood. Note the marble drinking fountain and its wrought-iron canopy.

Cottages in Mitford Street, Stretford, 1898. Not far away was the village pinfold where stray animals were kept until reclaimed on payment of a fine. In the nineteenth century, Stretford, in the Salford Hundred, had eight inns, comparable with Droylsden, Didsbury, Failsworth, Denton and Crumpsall.

Looking north down Wilmslow Road, Withington, 1908. Two strong horses pad along the wide, sett-paved road. These were needed for heavy loads such as bales of cotton, and for pulling brewers' drays. Trams ran frequently to the hospital.

The Pickering Arms, Thelwall, 1900. Carved on the inn's upper timbers is the inscription 'In the year 920 Edward the Elder founded a city here and called it Thelwall.' In the 1900s, cyclists were welcome and teas were provided at the Pickering Arms.

Leigh Market Place, 1910. In this busy market town, Collier's stall sold cotton and silks. The obelisk indicates where the town cross once stood. Leigh is associated with Thomas Tyldesley, who died at the Battle of Wigan Lane supporting King Charles.

Prescot Watches, 1918. This is a reminder that the skill of watch-making was introduced in 1595 by Huguenot refugees. In the eighteenth century, Prescot produced the best watch movements in England. Now the town has a Museum of Watch and Clock Making. This building became the 'Pals' Barracks'.

Gladstone Dock, Liverpool.

Gladstone Dock, Liverpool, mid-1930s. The first dock, built in the eighteenth century, made history in being a wet dock controlled by floodgates and set a pattern worldwide. Trade expanded so rapidly that more docks had to be constructed: George's Dock, Canning Dock, Prince's Dock, Queen's Dock, Coburg Dock and Gladstone Dock, named after the great Victorian statesman William Ewart Gladstone, who was born at 62 Rodney Street, Liverpool, on 29 December 1809. The most famous is Albert Dock, designed by engineer Jesse Hartley appointed by the Docks Board. It was opened in 1845 by Queen Victoria's husband, the Prince Consort, after whom it was named. Albert Dock was unique in having warehouses adjacent so that bales of cotton could be unloaded immediately the ships arrived. Eventually, Liverpool's dockland grew to 7½ miles of docks and warehouses.

The George's Landing Stage, Liverpool, *c*. 1936. The city waterfront remains famous, with Liverpool Pierhead dominated by the Royal Liver building, the Cunard building and the Dock Board offices. Ferries to Birkenhead, Seacombe and New Brighton started from George's Landing Stage.

Prince's Landing Stage, Liverpool, 1910. To this landing stage came all the great liners and boats for North Wales, Ireland and the Isle of Man. Overlooking it was the Titanic Monument, erected in memory of the engineers who were lost when the *Titanic* struck an iceberg on her maiden voyage to New York in 1912.

Royal Charter, luxury steam clipper, 1858. Returning to Liverpool from Australia and caught in a hurricane, this vessel was wrecked on the cliffs of Anglesey in October 1859 after covering thousands of sea miles and in sight of home. On board was a bullion cargo of £322,440 in gold bars and bags of gold dust. Passengers returning from the gold fields carried an estimated £150,000 in sovereigns. Describing the disaster in his weekly magazine *All the Year Round*, the Victorian novelist Charles Dickens wrote: 'Never was destruction so complete.' So tremendous was the force of the sea that it had beaten gold ingots into the ironwork of the vessel. With dawn came the miraculous sight of sovereigns drifting with the sand, scattered like sea shells in their hundreds. Four months' salvage work concentrated on recovering the gold. The wreck was sold for £1,000 and a further 500 sovereigns were revealed when *Royal Charter*'s stern post was lifted. Only £1,200 of passenger gold was surrendered to the Receiver of Wreck, but £30,000 of bullion was recovered. As recently as August 1970 a *Royal Charter* brass button was found at Moelfre Head, and the ship's signal gun adorns a Welsh lawn. Local families were said to become mysteriously rich. The wrecking of this clipper became one of the legends of the sea.

The Town Hall, Liverpool, 1920s. Built at the top of Water Street by John Wood of Bath, between 1749 and 1754, fifty years later it was damaged by fire and had to be reconstructed by James Wyatt, who added the dome and the Corinthian portico.

Liverpool Pageant, 1908. 'The Surrender of Liverpool' float represented the Cromwellian era when eighty Royalists were killed at Liverpool Castle in Col. Assheton's 1643 siege. It was King John who first encouraged settlers to the town of Liverpool in order to establish a royal borough.

Knowsley Hall, *c.* 1920. Since the fourteenth century the Earls of Derby lived at the hall situated 2 miles from the village of Knowsley. A safari park opened in 1971 and the landscaped grounds are now freely roamed by lions, giraffes and elephants.

Speke Hall, *c.* 1960. This fine half-timbered building, the home of the Norris and Watt families, and too close to Liverpool Airport for its well-being, was constructed in stages between 1500 and 1612. There is a royal bedroom where Charles I is thought to have slept in 1630.

Elegant Adelaide Terrace, Waterloo, *c.* 1900. This suburb of Liverpool, built about the time of the famous battle, was inhabited by wealthy Liverpool merchants. From its sands, visitors could view the Mersey shipping. The artist J.M.W. Turner came to paint its sunsets.

St Helen's, early this century. Tram No. 14 is about to pass Craddock's outfitters. The opening of a canal from St Helen's to Warrington in 1762 by the Sankey Navigation Company facilitated the transport of coal from this important Lancashire coalfield.

'The smallest house in England', Wavertree, near Liverpool, 1905. Incorporated into the city in 1895, Wavertree had fine brick Georgian houses, a clock tower memorial to Sir James Picton, a coaching inn, the Lamb Hotel and an interesting old lock-up dating from 1796. Wavertree Garden Suburb was developed under the guidance of the Liverpool Garden Suburb Tenants Ltd, the first hundred houses being completed by 1912. Perhaps with the smallest house in mind, no more than twelve houses to the acre were allowed, with adequate garden space.

St Philip's Church, Orrell Road, Litherland, 1908. This Victorian Gothic building with its eight-sided spire was consecrated in 1864. The site was provided by the Earls of Sefton, who also developed Aintree Racecourse. Construction of the Leeds and Liverpool Canal improved the town commercially, providing cheap transport for its goods, and in 1893 the Liverpool Overhead Railway made Litherland its terminus. Residential property was built, but prior to this development Litherland was little more than a village, the original settlement having been made by the Norsemen when they came to Lancashire's shores.

HARTLEY'S MARMALADE AND PRESERVE WORKS, AINTREE

A BIG and busy department, where every jar is washed, boiled and sterilized before it passes into the Filling Rooms.

Hartley's famous marmalade and preserve works, Aintree, 1920s. This department washed, boiled and sterilized every jar before its passage into the filling room. Mr W.P. Hartley began as a boy by persuading his parents to make and sell jam in their grocer's shop.

The King's statue, Bootle, 1914. This imposing monument honoured King George V following his coronation in 1910. It had been proposed by wealthy Liverpool merchants who had built houses along tree-lined Trinity Road. The earliest settlers were attracted by Bootle's springs of crystal-clear drinking water. The Saxon word, 'botl', from which the town gets its name, means 'dwelling'.

Market Day, Ormskirk, *c.* 1930. The cloth stall in Market Place is outside Draper's Café, at a time when Lancashire calico could be bought for 10d. a yard. Granted the right under an ancient charter to hold annual fairs on Whit Monday and Tuesday, Ormskirk grew in importance as a market town throughout the eighteenth century. The cheese and butter market was held beneath the old town hall, where weights and measures clerks were appointed to check the stalls. Busy Liverpool and Southport needed the produce sold on market days, and stagecoach passengers and traders from all around needed inns where they could refresh themselves or haggle over prices. More agricultural land for growing good crops of vegetables was made available by the drainage of Martin Mere.

John Aindow, lifeboatman, Formby, 1891. John was one of many members of his family to serve in saving life. In 1892 he was reappointed when a new boat came to the station and Mr Edward Jones, keeper of Crosby Lighthouse and Telegraph Station, was made superintendent. The crew then consisted of Robert Aindow snr, Robert Aindow jnr, Henry Rice, Henry Aindow, John Aindow, Joseph Aindow, Robert Aindow, Robert Eccles, John Eccles, John Brooks, Henry Brooks and Henry Aindow jnr. To pull out the lifeboat, Edward Sutton of Marsh Farm supplied strong horses at 9s. per horse, and the crew were paid 7s. 6d. a day for launching and exercise.

The old windmill, Crosby, 1907. This mill was situated in the parish of West Derby, 2 miles from Ormskirk, and by this time it had lost its sails. A century earlier the miller, John Wignall, was kept very busy in this mainly agricultural area.

Birchfield Road, Widnes, 1906. Advertising Sunlight Soap on its gable end, this shop was later the tuck shop for Wade Deacon Grammar School for boys, which was built opposite in 1931. In the pram is Charles Calvert.

St Michael's Church, Hough Green, near Widnes, 1905. To the left of the church was the vicarage, which became a nursing home. The infamous 'Hough Green Murder Stone' is behind the trees in the foreground.

Group from Huyton on a church outing, possibly to Sefton Park, 1908. Until recently, Huyton's church rang the curfew bell in winter months, as did the church of St Chad, Poulton-le-Fylde.

Upholland, now part of Skelmersdale and Holland, 1908. The so-called haunted house was situated next to the graveyard, and perhaps earned its reputation because the ruins of the Priory, built in the fourteenth century by Robert de Holland, may have been used in the building of houses and the church.

CENTRAL LANCASHIRE

Broadway, Rochdale, c. 1900.

The Bowling Green in the Park, Radcliffe, *c.* 1932. Early this century, Radcliffe, a town that grew up by a curve of the River Irwell, was ahead of some towns, with its Technical School and Public Swimming Bath. The fifteenth-century home of the Radcliffe family fell into ruin.

Peel Tower, Holcombe Hill. Holcombe Brook near Bury has long been well known for the 120 ft high Peel Tower built on the top of Holcombe Hill in the 1850s in honour of Sir Robert Peel, MP. Every Easter Monday it was traditional to walk up the 1,200 ft hill and climb the Tower.

The Lancashire and Yorkshire Railway Station, Bolton Street, Bury, 1930s. Opened in 1847, the station burned down a century later. Early this century the high level station served the line between Clifton Junction and Accrington, while the low level station catered for the line between Bolton and Rochdale.

Bury Jubilee Celebrations, 1926. This was the children's pageant, in which hundreds of children took part in an intricate assemblage, dressed to form the colours of the town's coat of arms. Famed for black puddings sold on Bury Market, the town had a popular coffee house on Walmsley Road. The market hall was built on the site of the old market cross.

Postcard of 1908 commemorating John Collier of Milnrow near Rochdale. Otherwise known as 'Tim Bobbin', a Lancashire dialect writer, John died on 14 July 1786 aged 75. His wife Mary died on 14 June of the same year. They were a well matched couple. The verse on his grave reads:

Here lies John and with him Mary,
Cheek by jowl and never vary.
No wonder that they so agree,
John wants no punch and Moll no tea.

Below is Tim's cottage by the River Roach, used in his day for handloom weaving, until the introduction of machinery reduced some weavers to total poverty. This led to riots and machine-breaking. In the early nineteenth century, weavers from Darwen, Mellor, Tockholes and Oswaldtwistle 'destroyed and burned engines erected by Mr Arkwright'. Ten thousand marched from Bolton, Blackrod, Wigan and Chorley once they heard of his invention. They smashed up his spinning-jenny at Stainhill near Blackburn and Richard fled, but eventually workers had to accept the revolutionary changes. Years later, James Schofield, flannel manufacturer, prospered at Milnrow.

'Knocker-up', Royton, 1905. At 5 a.m. this man would come round and tap on the millworkers' bedroom windows with his long pole to waken them in time for the 6.00 a.m. 'buzzer' at the mill. This was necessary as some had to walk long distances, and there were fines imposed for being even two minutes late.

The Cricket Ground, Heywood, July 1930. The ground is overlooked by the tallest mill chimney for miles. Within easy reach were the beauty spots Carr Wood, Ashworth Valley, Simpson Clough, Queen's Park, and Hopwood Hall with its Italian and rock gardens.

Market Square, Heywood, 1908. On 25 September 1928, Harold Pyott, who lived in Heywood for eight years, celebrated his forty-first birthday. He was acknowledged to be the smallest man in the world: 23 in tall, weighing 24 lbs. Periodically he toured all the principal fairgrounds.

W. H. MILLS,
DISPENSING & FAMILY CHEMIST,
1, Market Street, HEYWOOD.

OILS, PAINTS, AND COLOURS.
FRESH ROASTED COFFEE. GENUINE PATENT MEDICINES.
AGENT FOR THE LONDON TOWER TEA.
SODA WATER, LEMONADE, &c.
Sauces, Pickles, and Vinegars.

W.H. Mills, chemist, 1902. This shop sold a great variety of goods, including pickles and freshly roasted coffee. By 1883 the *Mills Heywood Family Almanack*, with a guaranteed circulation of 2,000, was in its twenty-fourth year of publication. Printed by Mr G.H. Kent of York Street, this general advertiser also emanated from the Mills' premises at 1 Market Street. At No. 3 was James Coombes, shoe repairers; No. 5 was the C.W.S. butchers; No. 7 Globe Mantles; No. 9 a shoe shop; and No. 11 Duckworth's grocer's shop.

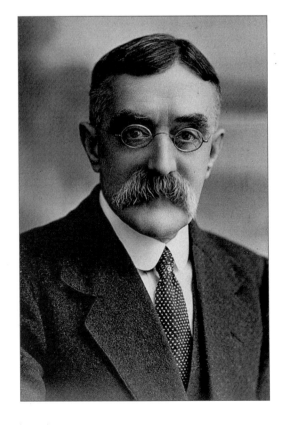

Mr W.H. Mills, born in the 1860s. Mills and his son Hubert were also photographers, and the shop was the agent for Kodak printing paper. In the long attic gallery at the top of the premises, grandson Fred amused himself by propping up used glass whole plates and firing his air rifle at them, an act since regretted all his adult life. Hubert refused to carry on the business, so, on retirement, Mr Mills sold out to Jesse Boot, chemist, on condition that the family continued to live above the premises. He left all of his money to Ashworth Chapel, Heywood.

Drake Street, Rochdale, 1906. The town, backed by the Rossendale Fells, takes its name from the River Roach. Toad Lane is where the Co-operative Movement was born in 1844. John Bright, champion of free trade, hailed from Rochdale, where his family had a cotton spinning mill.

MADAME PARSONS AND HER POPULAR FAMILY, INCLUDING THE 7 LITTLE LANCASHIRE LASSES, THE 2 LANCASHIRE LADS AND THEIR SOLDIER DADDY, SGT. PARSONS, A.O.C.

The Parsons family. Rochdale was the home of Madame Parsons and her family of entertainers: seven girls, two boys and father, Sgt Parsons. They performed in Lancashire theatres in the early 1900s. The girls could quickly change from ringlets and ribbons to clog dancing.

Albert Lee. This brave boy was drowned in the
River Roach while making a heroic attempt to
rescue his playmate on Saturday 15 June 1907.
Children made their own entertainment, some
proving dangerous. Mill lodges were used for
swimming, and there were fatalities because of the
depth, coldness and proximity to bleaching and
dyeing works. Such tragic deaths made news, as did
the murder of father and son 'Bill o' Jack's and Tom
o' Bill's' of Greenfield. Bell of Heywood and A. and
H. Hanson of Greenfield photographed the scene of
the crime. 'Such interest did their tragic end excite
that 'ere they were removed from human sight
thousands on thousands daily came to see.' The
father and son kept an inn, later called the
Moorcock, until their murder by two poachers in
1832.

David Ashworth. This was the friend of Albert Lee
who got into difficulties while swimming. Both
boys lived near Rochdale and would have known of
Rochdale Wakes Week when the fair arrived in
town with its hobby horses, quack doctors, pedlars,
wild beast show, circus with Buckskin Billy, Indians,
brandy snaps, black puddings, hot peas and 'lots of
things besides', as the 1890s verse 'Rachda Wakes'
puts it.

'A bit of old Littleborough', 1917. Next to the solid building with its flight of stone steps and cellars once used by hand-loom weavers is the Albert Hall. Sixteenth-century Stubbley Old Hall was the oldest building in Littleborough. On the way from Littleborough to Todmorden, cut into stone was the tariff for the toll road.

Far Chatterton and the Park at Ramsbottom, *c.* 1920. Ramsbottom grew from a hamlet into a busy town. The benevolent Grant brothers who established the hamlet were immortalized by novelist Charles Dickens in *Nicholas Nickleby*.

A Lancashire tea party, *c*. 1900. This was held in a garden that is now believed to be at Summerseat, which had a station on the old East Lancashire Railway line between Rawtenstall and Bury. Mr Lewis E. Hanson is in the group and the lady standing (left) was from Raikes Parade, Blackpool.

Bacup Auxiliary Firemen. This brigade served the Rossendale Valley during the Second World War, their headquarters being in Henrietta Street, Bacup. Mr James Hince of Waterfoot is present (seated front row, far right).

Typical Lancashire stone dwellings at Balladin, with the fells rising sheer behind, 1920. 'The Glen' through Pendle and Rossendale forests once abounded with vaccaries, or 'booths', where cattle were reared, for example Crawshaw, Goodshaw and Lower Booths. The name still persists. This photograph was taken by Mr E. Reed of Rawtenstall.

The premises of E. Taylor, Sons and Company Ltd, 36 Burnley Road, East Waterfoot, late 1940s. This shop sold wallpaper, paints and distempers, and the owners were prepared to take on house decorating. At the junction of Bacup Road and Burnley Road East was the shopping arcade built by Sir Henry Trickett, five times Mayor of Rawtenstall and the biggest shoe manufacturer in the area during the late nineteenth century. Sir Henry tried to make Waterfoot the most important shopping centre in the Rossendale Valley. The arrival of the railway led to the town's development.

Burnley Road, Rawtenstall, Rossendale Valley, 1920s. At this time a few motor cars had appeared. Because the hills rose immediately behind the town, in times of heavy rain, houses and mills could be flooded despite householders fixing floodboards at the back and front doors.

An outing from Newchurch-in-Rossendale arranged by the Newchurch Boot Company, 8 May 1909. All of these wagonettes were hired by the mill owners Walmsley, Taylor and Worswick Partners. The author's great-grandmother was a Worswick and might be among this happy, high-perched throng.

Market Street, Bacup, 1911. All the people in this busy street have their eyes focused on the photographer, who has brought the tram advertising Nubolic soap to a standstill. White dresses and hats and a black umbrella to protect the lady's complexion from the sun indicate that this is a summer scene. In the town centre stands St John's Church, which was built in 1880, with its fine stained-glass windows depicting saints and apostles. Parks that enrich the area, including Stubbylee and the Dell, afford good views of the moorlands rising behind the town. Remains of ancient fortifications, green mounds of Broadclough Dykes, lie between Bacup and Burnley. Here the Saxon battle of Brunaburgh may have been fought in the tenth century – it is one of many disputed sites. From Bacup in the Rossendale Forest a stretch of moorland can be traversed as far as spectacular and legendary Cliviger Gorge. One of Bacup's interesting links with the past is the Old Meadows Colliery, with its chain haulage system for drawing iron tubs along the colliery railway.

Bacup Amateur Operatic Society, just before the Second World War. In the centre behind the gentleman seated on the front row is dark-haired Phyllis Fielden of Waterfoot. One of a large family, the Fieldens moved to Edgeside when the estate was built in 1930.

Bacup station staff, 1900. The stationmaster (left), wearing the frock coat, is James Hince Snr, who was born in the 1850s. With provision for handling passengers, goods and livestock, the station also possessed a crane with a lifting capacity of 10 tons, one of the biggest around.

Morris dancers in the Helmshore Carnival procession. The event is attended by a policeman, and following the dancers are a brass band and Britannia mounted on a lorry. The Helmshore Fulling Mill and Higher Mill have been restored as the Museum of the Lancashire Textile Industry.

Musbury Church procession, 3 miles south-west of Haslingden, 1898. Haslingden Grane, Musbury Heights, Edgerton and Pickup Bank quarries were run by the firm of Hargreaves and Bolton. Some of the quarries' employees were in the procession.

Jubilee Road, Haslingden, 1930. Brownies, Sunday School scholars and ladies from St Stephen's Church join in hymn singing alongside their banner. The striped hut on the right was a popular chip shop on Grane Road.

The parish church of Atherton, 1936. This nineteenth-century church was known for its fine hammerbeam roof. The enterprising shop on the left advertised Cadbury's chocolate and Capstan cigarettes, and it ran a circulating library. Also in Atherton, Chowbent Chapel, which was built in 1721, had a three-decker pulpit above box pews. The chapel was built from the proceeds of a pension awarded to its nonconformist minister James Woods after the Jacobite Rebellion of 1715 when his son, heading eighty men armed only with pikes and scythes as weapons, held the passage of the River Ribble at Walton-le-Dale for the King's forces.

Park and Town Hall, Warrington, August 1910. A Georgian mansion designed by James Gibbs in 1750 originally for rich merchant Thomas Patten, this town hall expresses prosperity. The foundations consisted of copper slag from smelting works at Bank Quay. A settlement grew up east of Widnes before Roman times because the River Mersey could easily be forded.

The Barley Mow Inn, Warrington, 1907. Dating from 1561, this tavern is the oldest property in the town centre. Mullioned windows, black-and-white half-timbering in quatrefoil design and a seventeenth-century staircase within make this building a joy for the local historian.

Bridge Street, *c.* 1902. Warrington is one of Lancashire's oldest towns, the Angles having settled here in the seventh century. At Bridge Foot was established the famous Warrington Academy (1757–86). As dissenters could not attend universities, this academy founded by John Seddon, was the brilliant answer.

Warrington Bridge and New Wilderspool Bridge, early 1940s. The Romans built a fort at Wilderspool on the south bank of the Mersey, which they used as their industrial site. In the eighteenth century the 'Flying Stage Coach' left Warrington on Monday and arrived in London on Wednesday. The fare inside was 2 guineas.

The Conservative Hall, Haydock, late 1920s. In a mining town the church of St James stands out architecturally. A holy relic from the martyr Edmund Arrowsmith who was born at Haydock is preserved at Ashton-in-Makerfield.

The sale ring and jockeys' stand, Haydock Park, 1930. Haydock is a town well known for its horseracing. A century earlier, Kersal Moor and Heaton Park held race meetings.

Rayner Park, Hindley, *c.* 1930. The nineteenth-century church spire stands amid the mill chimneys of industrial Lancashire. John Leyland, a local benefactor, provided a library and a museum of miniatures.

The Central Wagon Company, 1960s. At Ince near Wigan the Central Wagon Company broke up condemned steam engines, although on a smaller scale than at Barrie Island 'graveyard'.

The Douglas Tavern, Chapel Lane, Wigan, early 1900s. The big central lamp was a meeting place in this important town. Nestle's milk, Post's cocoa, Brown's salt and other commodities were advertised on large posters on the gable end of the corner shop. Wigan was particularly famous for coal-mining, which began as early as 1450. One report states that 'the best coal in the universe' was in the middle of the town. There were twelve collieries digging 'cannel' coal, which was exported to America. The making of the Leeds and Liverpool Canal brought further prosperity. Wigan was linked to Leigh by a connection with the Bridgewater Canal, making it one of the most important industrial towns in the country. Bell founding, pottery, brass, pewter and iron forges were big business, and 'Wigan checks' were prized as being superior to those of Manchester. Clog-making flourished because of the heavy industry, sixty cloggers being listed in the 1910 *Wigan Directories*. Clog fighting or 'purring' was a Wigan way of settling arguments.

Market Place, Wigan, 1913. This bird's-eye view features trams, shop awnings and a large advert for Oxo, the housewife's standby when meat was scarce and expensive. Leading from Market Place are the medieval streets Wallgate, Standishgate and Millgate.

Wigan parish church, seen from Bishopsgate, 1901. The stones from a Roman altar are built into this ancient church. Sir William Bradshaw and his wife, Mabel, from the fourteenth century, occupy a tomb here. Poor Mabel had to do penance by walking barefoot to Wigan (Mab's) Cross. She had remarried, presuming William dead, when he failed to return from the Crusades after many years.

'Ye Olde Thatche', Eccles, 1909. Since 1893 Mr W. Wardle's shop had sold the original Eccles cakes made of flaky pastry filled with currants. The premises were much older than this. They were also famed for herb beer and home-made ice-cream. Next door was a shop that made baskets and cane chairs. Both properties were demolished in 1919.

Eccles Cross and horse trough, 1920. Church Street and the railway station are in the distance. The fragment of a Saxon cross was found when the canal was being cut. In 1961, Eccles Corporation bought the half-timbered Monks Hall, which was once connected with Whalley Abbey.

Lancashire's staple industry in No. 21 of the postcard series *Weavers at Work* features the mill at Kearsley in 1920. Inscribed on the back are cryptic lines about the girl weaver in the centre, Elsie Booth; Ernie states: 'This girl on Sunday, well, strangers would take her for the queen. She wears a duke's revenue on her back . . . and in her heart she scorns our poverty though she's but a weaver.' Elsie Booth was one of an army of thousands of cotton spinners and weavers. Horne and Hague of 2 Waterworth Street, Nelson, travelled through all of the cotton towns of Lancashire and recorded scenes: happy occasions such as birthdays; mill outings; coronations; Christmas time when the girls loved to fix decorations above the machinery – all opportunities for this photography firm.

Staff of George Tomlinson School, 1957. The school was named after the Minister of Education. Under its headmaster, Mr D. Berry front row (centre), the school earned an enviable reputation. He is flanked by deputy head Miss D. Redford and senior master Mr V.L. Atherton.

Nine Arches, close to the Viaduct Works, Earlestown, 1960. Earlestown, like Clitheroe, is well known for cement-making. Locomotives were made at the Vulcan foundry. From being a small chapelry known as Newton, by 1901 Earlestown's population had risen to 17,000, and is still growing because of the town's important nodal position.

Local gala, Little Hulton, c. 1930. This amusing float was one of many at this gala, where horsedrawn carts and drays were used for the tableaux. It belonged to a Little Hulton firm of builders and contractors. The photograph was taken by Mr W.E. Partington.

Visit to Smithills Hall, 1930. Mr C.E. Willis (far left), a photographer with premises at 87 Bradshawgate, Bolton, advertised an 'expert photographic service'. A mounted enlargement measuring 15 in by 20 in cost a mere 2s. 9d.

Ye Olde Man and Scythe, Bolton, 1904. The inscription on the inn wall reads: 'In this ancient hostelry James Stanley, 2nd Earl of Derby, passed the last few hours of his life previous to his execution, Wednesday 16 October A.D. 1651.'

Hall i' th' Wood, a mile from Bolton, 1908. In the eighteenth century this famous Tudor house was let as tenements. For a few shillings a week, poor people could have a room here, among them the inventor Samuel Crompton. Lord Leverhulme saved the hall from falling into complete ruin.

Firwood Fold, near Bolton, 1930s. A 'fold' was a settlement of cottages around a farmhouse. This one is famous as the birthplace of Samuel Crompton, the inventor of the spinning mule in 1780, which combined the ideas of the water frame and the jenny. Woollen yarns are still spun today on an improved form of mule. A bronze statue of Crompton was erected in Nelson Square, Bolton, but in his lifetime he was not adequately rewarded, his idea being stolen and he and his family continually having to struggle against poverty. A brilliant series of inventions by John Kay, Richard Arkwright, James Hargreaves, Edmund Cartwright and Samuel Crompton revolutionized the Lancashire cotton industry, but the long-established wool industry was less willing to try new ways.

The well-worn Sixty Three Steps at Barrow Bridge, near Bolton, 1930. By this time they had become part of a local beauty spot. In the nineteenth century this was originally a model industrial settlement motivated by Robert Gardner and Thomas Bazley, which carefully considered the educational, economic and social lives of the workers. Around 150 loaves were baked daily; meals were separate from mill surroundings; hot water and newspapers were provided; gas lighting and running water were available in the workers' back-to-back houses; and a workers' co-operative shop was established. The mill was closed in 1913 and the village deserted, but it has since been restored as a conservation area, a timely reminder of Lancashire's past.

Horwich, Winter Hey Lane, late 1930s. The Lancashire and Yorkshire Railway Company recognized the demand for better locomotives, and Horwich had the largest locomotive works in the world, constructed in 1888. This was a great change from the early community's engagement in farming, weaving and bleaching.

Great House Barn, Rivington, 1968. Rivington, meaning 'village of the mountain ash', had two great barns of Saxon foundation. In 1898 the manor was acquired by Viscount Leverhulme of Port Sunlight, who built a bungalow on Rivington Pike. Refreshments were available at the barn, to which many tourists flocked from industrial Lancashire. Mrs Elizabeth Gaskell is another famous name associated with Rivington, which she visited with her husband, a nonconformist minister. Rivington's inn, the Blackamoor's Head, was known locally as the Black Lad. Handloom weavers were beggared by the arrival of a weaving mill at Willow Beds. Some had to walk miles over the moors to reach Chorley or Adlington textile mills in time for clocking on at 6 a.m. Two Rivington farmers, Peter Shawe and George Smith, formed a partnership with a mining engineer, John Jowle, to mine lead ore on nearby Anglezark, but ownership problems led to strife and the deliberate flooding of the mine. Galena and copper were discovered in the eighteenth century, and later shell witherite, named after Dr Withering, which were used with galena as pottery glaze.

Mr S. Collier outside his clogger's shop, Westhoughton. This shop was typical of those to be found all over Lancashire, where almost everyone wore clogs. 'Clogger and boot repairer, hand-sewn work a speciality' – such craftsmen were indispensable. In the early 1900s, when new irons could be fitted for only 3d. a set, if it was Friday night, workers would either wait or leave the clogs for repair, run home barefoot, pick up the clogs the following morning and pay for them after work on Saturday when they received their wages. Some went to collect them at 'bell hour', that is dinner time. Like the small general store, the clog shop never seemed to close.

Chorley Town Hall, 1928. Henry Tate was born in Chorley in 1819 and began his working life as a grocer's assistant. He thought up a way of converting loaf sugar into cube sugar and eventually became the sugar king. With his wealth he created the famous Tate Gallery in London. The town has held a market since 1498 and at one time served all the farms in the area. As at Manchester, it held a 'Flat Iron' market on Tuesdays, based on the ancient practice of laying out goods for sale on the ground instead of using stalls. The fourteenth-century church of St Laurence is the oldest building in the town.

Market Street, Chorley, *c.* 1930. The town hall is in the distance. In early days, coal-mining, spinning, bleaching and printing cotton with water from the River Chor helped to establish the town, but Chorley was a market town in the thirteenth century.

This lady may have been housekeeper at Astley Hall, between Chorley and Euxton. With her lace, black satin, boned bodice, ringleted hair and large cameo on her left wrist, she typifies the mid-Victorian era. Originally a half-timbered dwelling built around a courtyard, the hall is a three-storey Jacobean house that was restored in the seventeenth century. The frontage of the building was pulled down and rebuilt in the grand style. The Charnocks of Charnock Richard had lived there in the sixteenth century because Charnock Hall had been burned down. After Thomas Townley Parker died in 1906 the building went to R. Arthur Tatton, who gave the hall and surrounding parkland to Chorley Corporation in 1922.

Leyland May Day Procession, Towngate, 1903. This event was a very old tradition passed down from the days of Guisings, when country people would usher in the spring when manorial rents were due. The procession then accompanied a garlanded frame hung with ribbons, flowers and silver to make a brave show. A 'king' and a 'fool on a hobby horse' also attended.

St Andrew's Parish Church, *c.* 1900. The town of Leyland, famed worldwide for the manufacture of lorries and buses, could also harness a donkey to a lawn mower. At St Andrew's Church, the curate prepared to mow and roll the graveyard with a little help from Neddy.

COTTON TOWNS

The Easter Parade, Avenham Park, Preston, 1909.

Preston Guild, the Trades' procession, Textile Trades and Cotton Arch, 1922. The famous week-long Preston Guild has been held every twenty years since the sixteenth century. Samuel Horrocks's first mill for spinning cotton was followed by many more, and with the cotton boom the population increased enormously.

Tulketh Mills, Preston, 1925. At this time the chimney of G. Reed and Sons, 123 Corporation Street, was in need of repair. To haul up scaffolding and staging to such a height must have been a challenge to the steeplejacks.

Preston Free Library, early 1900s. Now known as the Harris Public Library, Museum and Art Gallery, this building was constructed between 1882 and 1893, an expression of true civic pride, upholding the town's motto 'Proud Preston'. 'To Literature, Arts and Sciences' is carved beneath an imposing pediment supported by massive Ionic pillars. In the foreground is all the bustle of a traditional pot fair. The County Sessions House built in 1903, the war memorial in Market Square designed by Sir Giles Gilbert Scott, and the Georgian architecture of imposing town houses in Winckley Square were indicative of a prosperous town. Preston's history, however, stretches much further back. Street patterns and names such as Friargate, Stoneygate and Fishergate indicate a medieval past. Long a centre of commerce, it received the right to hold a Guild Merchant in Henry II's reign. Lying at the very heart of Lancashire, Preston has traditionally been the administrative centre of the county and was represented in parliament as far back as the thirteenth century.

The Preston Docks dredger *Astland* was holed when it ran aground in the channel at Lytham on 17 January 1961. In the background a cargo ship passes on its way to Preston Docks while *Astland* is being examined by divers.

Fulwood Barracks near Preston, 1904. The splendid arch has gone, but the lion and unicorn were placed on the ground with a record of the original cost down to the last farthing. The site of the barracks was the old Roman road on which stand Ribchester and Kirkham.

Penwortham Bridge, 1906. This bridge carries the road from Preston to Liverpool. An earlier bridge was built higher up river in 1706, which comprised five segmental arches and passing places. This area abounds with history, including stirring battles, a Norman castle and a Celtic fort.

London, Midland and Scottish Railway locomotive 4056 pulling seven coaches, Skew Bridge, Penwortham, between Farington station and Preston, July 1925. All holiday excursion trains carried boards at the front such as this, No. 860, to facilitate identification.

Hutton Grammar School Cricket 1st XI, 1937. The team captain, A.M. Maguire (front row, centre) was awarded the Military Medal and Military Cross during the Second World War, and subsequently became a QC. The school, founded in 1552, always maintained a high academic and sporting tradition.

The Rectory, Croston *c.* 1919. The rectory was at this time the residence of the Bishop of Whalley. He was acquainted with Dr T.D. Whittaker of 'The Holme', who wrote *A History of the Parish of Whalley,* and was concerned in the excavations of Whalley Abbey.

Moss's Cotton Weaving Mill, Kirkham, early 1900s. In charge was the man at the back, who was known as the 'Gaffer'. In 1926 the girls gave a party for 'Owd Kitty', who had worked there for sixty years. Every year all the factories in Preston and Kirkham closed down for Wakes Week.

Thatched cottages and the windmill, Wrea Green, August 1902. Visitors came in wagonettes to view the village and to eat strawberries and cream at the Grapes Inn. The only Fylde village with a duck pond, it is now a commuters' haven.

St Andrew's Church, Ashton-on-Ribble, 1911. This postcard was produced for the benefit of visitors. A dormitory suburb, like Fulwood and Grimsargh, Ashton's housing developments were popular with office workers in Preston's administrative centre.

The Bamber Bridge Girls' Friendly Society, forming part of a Whitsuntide procession from St Saviour's Church, *c*. 1900. The girls are passing the walls of Cuerden Park. Almost a century earlier a hoard of treasure was found not far away at Cuerdale, possibly hidden by a retreating army. Was the battle of Brunaburgh fought there? Some think so.

The Unicorn Inn, Walton-le-Dale, 1901. The River Darwen, mentioned in a poem by blind John Milton, flows under the bridge to join the Ribble. Cromwell slept at the Unicorn Inn in 1648 when Scottish rebels marched south to join the Royalists; the bloody three-day Preston Fight ensued. The Cromwell Association put up a plaque at what became the Unicorn Café: 'Battle of Preston – from this site Oliver Cromwell directed the battle and led the Parliamentary Army to victory that ended the second Civil War.' Butcher's Brow nearby denotes the terrible slaughter of fleeing Scottish soldiers. The loyal squires of Lancashire, including Thomas Tyldesley, who regularly galloped over on horseback, held secret meetings at the inn to drink to 'the king over the water' when the Stuarts were in exile. Walton-le-Dale's church set high on an eminence 80 ft above the Ribble was a wonderful look-out in times of trouble. On its walls can still be traced sixteenth-century masons' marks.

Grand reunion of the Brown family of Lostock Hall, Bamber Bridge, Leyland and Farington, Lostock Hall, May 1954. After the First World War, when jobs in Britain were scarce, two of the sons, Jack and Harold, emigrated to America. For a time they worked for the Canadian Pacific Railway. After thirty-five years, Jack sailed with his wife Nellie back to Liverpool to be met by members of the family, but Harold never returned. Back row, left to right: Eddie Rothwell, Ronald Ingham, Ernie Tomlinson, Edwin Rothwell, Ernest Tomlinson, Frank Brown, Harold Brown, Kenneth Ingham and Tom Brown. Second row: Sydney Warren, Joan Ingham, Joan Ingham, Edward Ingham, Dorothy Brown, May Brown, Nellie Brown, Dorothy Brown and Edna Warrenn. Third row: Annie Tomlinson, Fred Brown, Lucy Bamber, Jack Brown, Nellie Brown, Rose Brown, Ada Rothwell and Alice Ingham. Front row: Catherine Rothwell (author), John Rothwell, Stella Rothwell, Kathryn Warren, Kathleen Ingham and Michael Ingham.

Aerial view of Hoghton Tower, early this century. The tower dates from 1565. In the Banqueting Hall on 17 August 1617, King James I, having enjoyed a tasty meal, 'knighted' a loin of beef with the words, 'Arise Sir Loin!'. In the eighteenth century, Hoghton village was the centre of handloom weaving and the then almost derelict Hoghton Tower was let out to weavers in tenements.

Brindle, near Whittle-le-Woods, *c.* 1920. The parish church of St James dates back to the fifteenth century. Brindle held steeplechases, usually in April, in fields behind the church, to which 20,000 people turned up in 1905.

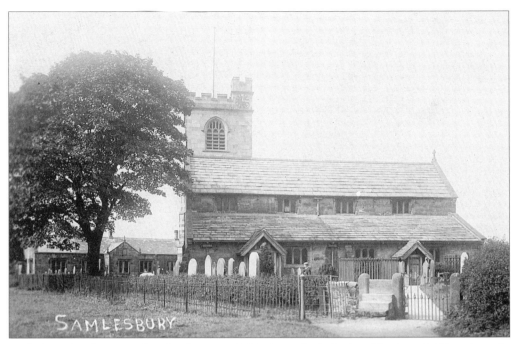

Samlesbury church, 1900. This church is set in fields alongside the banks of the River Ribble, where the foundations of the old hall can still be traced. A mile away is the famous black-and-white, half-timbered Samlesbury Hall, one of the most famous in Lancashire.

'A photograph of the old toll bar at Mellor taken on the day it was closed, November 1st 1890.' On this postcard full of history, note, from left to right, the old milestone '7 miles to Preston from Mellor', the water butt and the toll-keeper's hut looking like a sentry box.

Longridge, Coronation Day, June 1953. A group of excited children waved flags for Queen Elizabeth (pictured in the shop window behind them). News that Sir Edmund Hillary and Sherpa Tenzing had climbed Everest was held back until the great day dawned.

Ribchester Bridge over the River Ribble. The bridge was built in 1774. Nearby a ceremonial bronze helmet, now in the British Museum, was found. Other Roman discoveries included a ring, its cornelian stone engraved with a raven and the words: 'Greetings to thee whom I love as dear as my life.'

Nurses at Whittingham, near Preston, early this century. The large psychiatric hospital had its own railway system and farms to supply the vast quantities of food necessary for feeding thousands of patients. One can be certain that the nurses are clad in Hoyle's F Cloth, made in Lancashire, which had 'a worldwide reputation for nurses' uniforms, continuous for over half a century'.

Goosnargh, early 1900s. Isaac Ball stopped his Model T Ford to inspect one of his steam traction engines, which had been hired out for road mending. From his stock yard at Wharles he also leased tar sprayers and baling machines.

Billington, near Clitheroe, 1901. A horse and trap was useful for travelling between villages. The well-wooded Ribble Valley reflected purely pastoral scenery, yet not far away were busy cement and textile mills. One of Robin Hood's men, Guy of Gisborne, was born near Billington.

The Spring Bridge over the River Hodder at Whitewell, near Clitheroe, *c*. 1900. Amid this wooded area, encircled by hills and beloved by fishermen and walkers, was the Whitewell Hotel, the last licensed house for the traveller through the Trough of Bowland.

The North-east Gateway, Whalley Abbey

Whalley Abbey's North-East Gateway, *c.* 1930. The abbey was established by a body of 'white monks' or Cistercians in 1296. The name derives from Cisteaux in Burgundy, where the order was instituted 200 years before. Whalley Abbey was not consecrated until 1306, and for many years building continued. Dr Whittaker, Vicar of Whalley, wrote: 'They adorned the site with a succession of magnificent buildings . . . they protected tenants, educated and provided for children, employed, clothed and fed many labourers, herdsmen and shepherds.' Only gateways, fragments of walls, arches and windows remain. The buildings covered about 6 acres and the enclosed grounds 36 acres.

King Street, Whalley, 1900. On the left was Pollard's Fancy Depository, and further up the road was the Whalley Arms Inn. Stagecoaches came through this township situated close to Clitheroe, which was possibly founded by the Romans to connect with Ribchester. A cycle of Mystery plays was presented in June 1996 to celebrate 700 years of Whalley Abbey.

Whalley Road, Clayton-le-Moors, near Accrington, 1909. Many of the townspeople found employment at the Canal Saw Mills or in calico printing. As at Great Harwood, all the cotton mills have now gone. Tudor Sparth Manor, Clayton, has mullioned windows and a projecting porch of two storeys.

Downham village near the Lancashire and Yorkshire Railway Station at Chatburn, 1905. In the background is Pendle Hill, once the haunt of the notorious Lancashire Witches. Three bells are said to have been brought from Whalley Abbey and hung in the tower of Downham church. The font was given by the last Abbot of Whalley.

St Mary's Church Sunday School procession, Clitheroe, *c.* 1920. This procession was part of the Whit Week Walks throughout the town. Historic Clitheroe held ox-roastings and pageants. The banner from Low Moor (dubbed 'Pig City' because the villagers ate so much bacon) was embroidered with a pig.

Isabel Wilkinson (left) and friend outside Mrs Wilkinson's home, West View, Clitheroe, 1900. The house, built of good Accrington brick, cost £200 to build. Mr Garnett of 'Shireburn' lent the money to a trusted workman, who paid it back in instalments. The Garnett family, mill owners like those at Barrow Bridge, provided simple cottages for their employees. Daily newspapers were available in a reading room. There was no running water in the 'one up and one down' cottages, but there were four bathhouses. Lavatories were in blocks of six at the top of New Row, Cross Street and Eastwood Place. St Anne's Square, where the village school stood, was known as 'up tip' because rubbish was deposited there.

The Taylor family outside their home at Low Moor, near Clitheroe, 1897. Back row, left to right: Esther, Alice Ann, Edith, John and Luke (killed in the First World War). Middle row: Mary, Mrs Alice Taylor, Mr Luke Taylor, Martha and Emma. Front row: Sarah, Charles, Laura, Tom (killed in the First World War) and Elizabeth (100 years old at the time of writing). Emma, in button boots, wears a beautiful handmade lace collar. Luke Taylor Snr, who was a spinning master, worked all of his life at Low Moor Mill, which was owned by the Garnett family, and most of his fourteen children worked there too. Born in 1849, he died of food poisoning on 8 September 1921. Granny Alice Taylor, Miss Wilkinson before marriage, took the post to Stonyhurst College. Three times a week she walked all of the way accompanied by her numerous brood. People came from the Waterloo area of Clitheroe to work at the mill: weavers, winders, tacklers, doffers, reachers and spinners. Six days a week they clattered in their clogs down Railway Road, Bawdlands, on to Edisford Road, through Giles Hitchen's Wood to Low Moor. It was said that as long as you could hear the clatter of clogs you were not late, and indeed it was a great clatter for between three and four hundred people were employed at the mill. A bakehouse in Union Street made bread and pies and was 'open all hours'. Long before the days of fish and chip shops, a lady in Albert Street, 'Old Liza' (Mrs Crabtree), made chips for the workers – a bowlful for 1d.

Grindleton village, May 1906. This was one of many villages in the picturesque Ribble Valley. At this time, followers of the otter hounds were seen along the River Hodder, and Lord Ribblesdale's pack hunted fallow deer at the end of the Trough of Bowland.

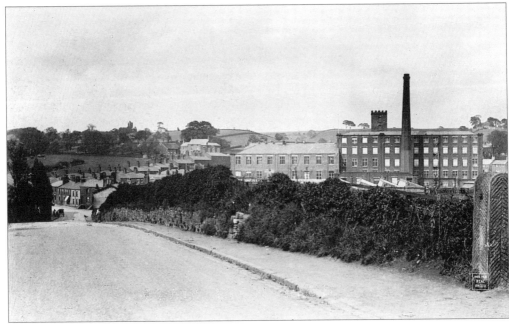

Black Lion Brow, Wheelton village 1927. As at White Coppice and Heath Charnock near Adlington, steep streets look down towards the Leeds and Liverpool Canal, that main artery which brought coal and was later extended to Whittle-le-Woods and Walton Summit.

Aftermath of a great mill fire, Darwen, 10 August 1920. Photographers came in force to record the disaster, and postcards were on sale within hours of the event. Throughout Lancashire there were many such conflagrations, because cotton yarn and cotton waste were so flammable.

The Hornby Statue seen from Sudell Cross, Blackburn, 1919. The YMCA advertised a concert on 3 April, while, where the handcart is parked (left), the Central Garage had recently opened to serve the few motor cars in town.

Whitsuntide procession, Great Harwood, 4½ miles north-east of Blackburn, 1916. Every branch of St Hubert's Church was represented in this well-ordered procession: clergy, churchwardens, bible class, Sunday Schools, Boys' Brigade and Girl Guides. Dressed in white, the older girls helped to steady the large silk banners by holding cords.

Great Harwood viewed from Edge End, 1915. The bleak Lancashire industrial towns had a quick escape to the surrounding hills and countryside. The mill workers, keen walkers and community singers, displayed comradeship, especially when times were hard.

Blackburn Town Hall and Market Place, 1945. In 1969 the Lord Lieutenant of Lancashire opened a fourteen-storey extension to the town hall, joining the nineteenth-century building with a glass-walled bridge. The famous contralto singer, Kathleen Ferrier, lived in Blackburn for twenty years.

Blackburn Market, early this century. Hartley's stall displays potatoes, tomatoes, chestnuts and apples, all at unbelievable prices. At the far left, in a peaked cap, stands market inspector Jonathan Cronshaw Hoghton.

Billinge End, near Blackburn, early this century. Tram No. 64, advertising Nestlé's Milk, stands at the corner of Preston New Road and Revidge Road. The Stork Hotel at Billinge is said to be haunted by the ghost of a swashbuckling Cavalier.

Close Brow, Rishton, Easter 1919. This scene shows the close proximity of countryside to industry. In the early nineteenth century, James and Richard Grimshaw were Rishton cotton manufacturers.

Blackburn Road, Church, near Accrington, 1950s. Many of the cotton mills date back to the Industrial Revolution. Calico printing was introduced by Sir Robert Peel's uncle. The town got its name Church from a place of worship connected with ancient Whalley Abbey.

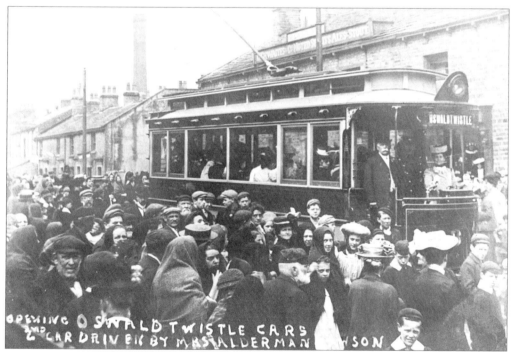

Opening of a tram car service to Oswaldtwistle, 2 August 1907. The second tram was driven by Alderman Mrs Rawson, an ex-mayoress. Calico printers Brooks and Company and Simpson Hough and Company provided most of the employment in Oswaldtwistle.

The Bandstand, Padiham, *c.* 1925. The bandstand was situated in the Memorial Park, which also had a museum and a rose garden. This mining town provided several parks, and Fenny Fold, a wooded valley, was another attraction. Padiham church has a 400-year-old font, which was presented by Abbot Paslew of Whalley Abbey.

Procession, Huncoat, 1930. The event enjoyed enormous crowd support. The first lorry features 'The Rock of Ages', prepared by Huncoat Wesleyan Sunday School, while the horsedrawn flat cart behind displays a poster that reads: 'Girl Guides Be Prepared'.

A steam tram car of the Baltic Fleet, Accrington, 1907. Note the old-fashioned uniform of the tram driver and the ubiquitous advertisement for Nestlé's milk. From 3,000 in the early eighteenth century, Accrington's population had grown to 45,000 by 1911.

Frank Davis, a local Accrington character, masquerading as Ben Hur in his mock-up chariot drawn by two donkeys. This was probably at the time when the film of that name appeared. The significance of SPQR may be a reference to the Latin, 'Senatus Populusque Romanus', meaning the Senate and Roman people. Alternatively, it may stand for, 'Small Profits and Quick Returns.' Whatever the meaning, the general air of merriment is unmistakable.

RUINS OF FIRE AT OWD TAT'S . ROGGERHAM.

Aftermath of fire at Roggerham, January 1906. This disastrous fire occurred on the moors near Padiham. How people loved to be photographed and to revel in an event, even though this one was 'Owd Tat's' misfortune. On such occasions it was customary for Lancashire people to have a 'whip round' for the unfortunate victim.

The opening of Towneley Hall, Burnley, 30 May 1903. Lord Roseberry opened the hall in front of vast crowds. This turreted mansion, home of the Towneley family, became Burnley's Museum and Art Gallery. A 6 ft thick wall hides a priest hole, its floor made of wattle, daub and rushes.

Robert Munn's chemist and druggist shop, St James Street, Burnley, Munn's Corner, 1900. Munn was also Registrar of Births, Marriages and Deaths for Burnley District. Next door was Carter's Dining Rooms, which also offered a bed for the night.

Two cannons from the Crimean War, brought back to Burnley as special mementoes for 'The Jubilee', 8 September 1855. To discourage boys from sitting on them, strong iron railings were ordered by the corporation. Burnley's St James Street had shops ranging from Dean's Drapers to a Colliery and Mill Furnishers with showrooms on two floors.

A formidable-looking lady from Clitheroe, *c*. 1914. This lady is believed to have been a nurse at Burnley General Hospital. Strict rules prevailed for the behaviour of both patients and nurses. Hours were long and work arduous in an atmosphere of carbolic and iodine. Such ladies did sterling work in two world wars. Burnley had a Market Charter in the thirteenth century and the right to hold an annual fair. In 1922 this included an enormous merry-go-round on the cattle market, where Gypsy Rachel told fortunes. During Burnley Fair Week in 1942 the 'Capital of the Pennines' ran agricultural shows and 'stay at home holiday attractions' in keeping with wartime austerity. Music was provided by the Band of the East Lancashire Regiment.

The picturesque packhorse bridge at Wycoller, 1960. Now a country park near Nelson and Colne, the village fell into ruin when handloom weavers could no longer make a living. Wycoller Hall was the model for Charlotte Brontë's Ferndean Manor in her novel *Jane Eyre*.

The waterfall at Barrowford, late 1960s. Near Foulridge, this was a farming community before textiles took over. Barrowford Toll House, built 1805, on the Marsden to Gisburn turnpike road, and a sixteenth-century packhorse bridge attract today's tourists. This photograph was taken by Shirley Page.

Brierfield, brass band. Like so many Lancashire towns, Brierfield formed a brass band in the nineteenth century. It performed at processions and Jubilee celebrations in the neighbouring towns. When coal was discovered at Little Marsden, three pits added to Brierfield's prosperity and cotton became the main source of employment.

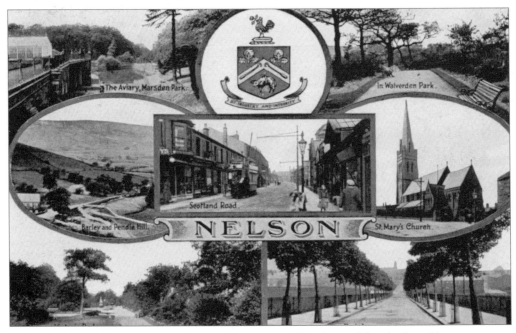

Seven scenes from Nelson in 1917 for Pte Peter Hayes, a soldier destined for Flanders. This cotton town had 30 acres of parks. The spired nineteenth-century St Mary's Church has eleven fine bells and two windows designed by Pre-Raphaelite artist Burne-Jones. 'By Industry and Integrity' is the town's motto.

Local wedding, 1908. The bride was a cousin of the Taylor family from Clitheroe. Hours of work went into tailoring, dressmaking and millinery. Many young girls 'went sewing' if they proved too frail for heavy mill work. This photograph was taken by K. Barrill of 4 Pendle Street, Nelson.

Wedding group from Fence, near Burnley, 1889. This studio, completed in 1885, with heavy brocade curtains and aspidistra plant, was the setting for champion cyclists and boxers with their trophies, miners in working gear, proud parents with babies, and cotton spinners in clogs. The backcloths were altered to fit the occasion.

Market Street, Colne, 1780. This engraving shows the Red Lion Inn from where the mail coach set out. At about this time a cloth hall was built by rich merchants to display their woollen garments. Colne was the birthplace of W.P. Hartley, who had the large preserve works in Liverpool.

Church Street, Colne, 1890. There was a coaching stop at the King's Head. Shaw's Tea and Coffee Rooms, specializing in Lipton's tea, were within easy reach of Sutcliffe's Corner. R. Chester, glazier, was on the corner by Shaw's leading into Cloth Hall Yard.

COUNTY TOWN, RURAL
AND HOLIDAY LANCASHIRE

Williamson Park, Lancaster, 1925.

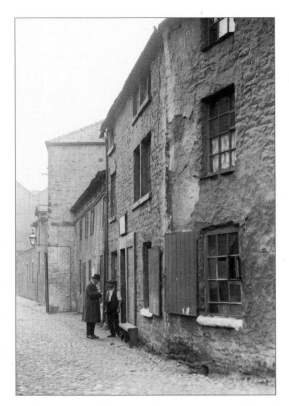

Damside Street, Lancaster, 1927. The old system of cobbled courtyards and streets persisted in Lancaster until 1960. Stone steps, galleries, iron railings, gas lamps and pumps remained, along with other signs of an ancient town, for example 'J. Patterson, Implement Maker and Coppersmith'. East Court had a communal tap in the yard and a sink at ground level. In 1850, Lancaster was the county town of the leading textile county, Lancashire, which then contained 1,235 cotton factories, 37 woollen and worsted factories, 9 flax factories and 29 silk factories, which totalled 15 million spindles, 185,000 power looms and 240,000 employees, of whom 130,000 were females and 12,000 were below the age of thirteen years.

Bridge Lane, Lancaster, c. 1920. At this time traffic was still mainly horsedrawn. A metal horseshoe in the road at Horse Shoe Corner, still visible today, indicates the site for horse fairs, of which Lancaster had a great number. Old China Lane had registered lodging houses run by Mr Scott. Winders Court, Cheapside and St Leonard's Gate were also part of old Lancaster. Penny Bridge, built when Lancaster Canal was constructed, expresses the history of an ancient town – a settlement chosen by the Romans. The canal company's horses were sold in Prince William Henry Field on 9 September 1842. On 14 November of the previous year the Lancaster Canal froze. The *Lancaster Gazetteer* chronicled all news, its first pages, numbering only four, appearing on 20 June 1801 from Benson's Court.

The Department of Chemistry, University of Lancaster, housed in the Faraday Building, 25 July 1973. The research student, John Rothwell, resided in County College on the campus. Designed by Bridgwater, Shepheard and Epstein, from its inception in 1963/4, the university became one of the city's major employers. By 1990 there were 9,315 students representing 90 nationalities. Under Vice-Chancellor Prof. Harold J. Hanham, the academic staff now number 1,088. The Nuffield Theatre, 'a superbly equipped and highly flexible space', runs three seasons of plays, dance and music coinciding with the university terms. Among the major international artists who have appeared in concert in the Great Hall are Yehudi Menuhin, Julian Bream, John Dankworth, and the Hallé and BBC Northern Orchestras. The university is sited at Bailrigg (Baylerig and Ballrigge being ancient derivatives), denoting a ridge with an expanse of woodland. The mansion, Bailrigg, was built in 1900 in Elizabethan style by Isaac Dilworth of Wavertree for a Lancaster merchant, Mr H.L. Storey. At nearby Quernmore, many ancient artefacts have been found, resulting in the university archaeological unit located in a restored Victorian building in the city.

The parish church of Lancaster, St Mary's Priory Church, standing high above the River Lune, 1912. When alterations were made that year, Roman lamps bearing Christian signs were unearthed and are now in Lancaster Museum. As it became the parish church in 1440 it escaped closure when the monasteries were dissolved.

Engraving showing a train leaving Lancaster Castle station for Preston, *c.* 1850. South of the station the Lancaster and Carlisle Railway joined the route of the Lancaster and Preston Junction Railway, the two lines having amalgamated. In the background is the castle and the priory church. Later the station was extended and the track layout was redesigned.

Baines Brothers' barge No. 35 makes its way along the Lancaster Canal in the Galgate area, *c.* 1900. Life was particularly hard for the ladies, who had to help with the work on board as well as bring up the children.

The City of Liverpool at Glasson Dock near Lancaster. A wet dock was built by the Lancaster Port Commissioners in 1787 as the Port of Lancaster was silting. They also built ten cottages to accommodate the shipyard workers. This became known as Ten Row.

Claughton near Kirkby Lonsdale, 1956. The bell on the right, dated 1296, is the oldest dated church bell in England. Nearby is the base of an ancient stone cross. Clay from the brickworks crossed the road in overhead wagons.

Woodgate Farm, Bleasdale. This farm was bequeathed to John Parkinson on 1 May 1815. His eldest son, Richard, became Canon Parkinson, famous for his book *The Old Church Clock*. When Queen Victoria visited Manchester in 1851, the canon gave £1,000 towards refurbishing Manchester Cathedral.

Garstang High Street, 28 June 1911. American millionaire, Mr Prescott Bigston, changes horses outside the Eagle and Child, which was run by the Richardson family. He was touring England in a coach and four with all the authentic touches from a century past, including the post horn.

Woodacre Hall Farm, Grizedale Valley, 1920s. This farm was once connected with John Rigmaden, master forester of Quernmore. The Revd Isaac Ambrose, while vicar of Garstang, built a house in Woodacre Wood, where he prayed and meditated.

Garstang morris dancers, Calder Vale in the Bowland area, June 1990. The dancers joined in the annual Calder Vale procession, carrying traditional morris sticks and wearing white socks and shoes.

The annual Royal Lancashire Show, early this century. Two chairmakers employed at Berry's Chairworks, Chipping, demonstrate their skills in making rush-bottomed chairs, which became famous beyond Britain's shores.

The cross at Churchtown near Garstang, early this century. Pot fairs were held around the cross. The twelfth-century church of St Helen was once the parish church of Garstang, so it became known as Churchtown as opposed to Garstang market town.

Great Eccleston village, near Poulton-le-Fylde, *c.* 1904. In early days, rush-light making from rushes growing by the River Wyre was a local industry. The rush cart brought fresh supplies quarterly for strewing in the churches, and the ceremony became a thanksgiving occasion attended by men performing the 'Long Morris'.

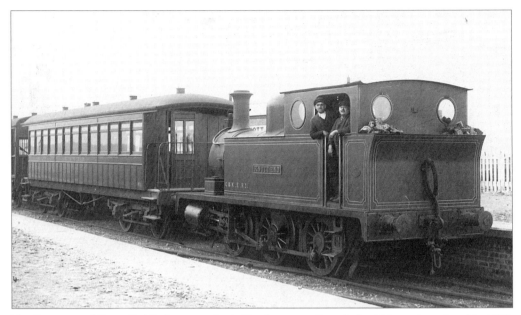

The Garstang and Knott End Railway train hauled by the engine *Knott End*, which was introduced in 1908. The locomotive *Farmer's Friend* was known as the 'Pilling Pig' because of its shrill whistle resembling the sound made by a dying pig. Other engines were *Blackpool, New Century* and *Jubilee Queen*, which appeared in 1899.

Salt mine workers at Preesall, Over-Wyre, 1900. Back row, left to right: Bob Myerscough, Jim Porter, Joe Danson, Jack Fairhurst, Bill Davis and Ted Wilson (boss). Front row: Bill Hodgkinson, Jim Whittaker (killed down the mine), Tom Johnson, Harry Barrow, Jack Johnston and Jack Parson; the last two are unknown. Mining had to be stopped because of serious subsidence.

Stalmine post office, Over-Wyre, 1906. Some years earlier the building was an inn. In 1895 there were nineteen farms in this agricultural area, many under family names from generations past, such as Buck's Farm; Roe's; Hudson's; Johnson's; Hankinson's. Lane names often derived from people, for example Old Tom's Lane and Green Dick's.

Hambleton, near Blackpool, early this century. This was a typical Fylde village of whitewashed, thatched cottages, famous for 'Hambleton Hookings', a large species of mussel which was hooked out of the River Wyre and became a sought-after delicacy until supplies disappeared in the early 1920s.

Opening of the Guide hut on Station Road, Poulton-le-Fylde, 1942. The hut was bought for £10, but much more was spent on improvement. Left to right: Miss K. Haslam (lieutenant), Mrs Williams, Tom Huddleston (council chairman), May Smithies and the district commissioner. When the ninth birthday of the 1st Poulton Rangers was celebrated here, the Revd Mr Fogg cut the cake.

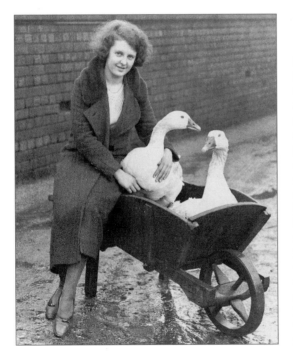

Kathleen Haslam with two geese outside Poulton-le-Fylde Auction Mart at the Christmas Stock Sale, 1932. On 'flesh day' during the week before Christmas, when thousands of geese, ducks, turkeys, cockrels and 'baby beef' were on sale, the whole of Market Square was filled with stalls. For centuries, Poulton served the surrounding countryside and Blackpool catering establishments when the holiday resort was bursting with visitors, some of whom had to find lodgings in Poulton. Easter was also a busy time for food sales, and, traditionally, when Lent was over, Poulton bakers presented their customers with an almond confection and at Christmas with the 'Yule loaf', a sweetmeat shaped like a manger, containing minced meat. In those days, chopped vine fruits were not used. However, this custom gradually died out in the nineteenth century.

The stocks and whipping post, Market Place, Poulton-le-Fylde, 1900. Stone.setts had in part replaced the cobblestones brought from the shore, about which villagers had complained so bitterly as being punishing to the feet. On the right is the printer's and bookseller's shop of Mr Lawrenson, who later worked from the tithe barn. The lamp was erected to mark Queen Victoria's Jubilee in 1891. Facing the stocks was Sir Alexander Rigby's town house (not shown) , and at the far end of the square was the Cyclist's Rest, which later became a bank. On this site centuries ago had stood the Moot Hall, but by 1910 all buildings around the churchyard were pulled down and a strong retaining wall erected. Some elegant town houses remain, for Poulton was a popular centre, but shops were taking over. The establishments shown here are a tailor, confectioner, dairy and tobacconist. In the distance, thatched cottages on Church Street are still in evidence, an area that seventy years later was to lead to the Teanlowe Shopping Centre, its name, though misspelt, deriving from yet another ancient Poulton custom, Teanlay Night, when bonfires burned at Compley.

J. Parkinson's, Great Carleton, early this century. This was an example of a village shop that sold everything from paraffin and firelighters to treacle and milk. It was also the village post office and was run by the same family for generations.

Performance at the Empire Day parade, Singleton, 1932. The now nostalgic *Masque of Empire*, organized by Mrs Wadsworth, involved a march past by more than 500 Girl Guides. The Revd W.S. Mellor of Poulton was present and Mrs P. Birley of Wrea Green took the salute.

Staining School, *c.* 1906. Teachers trained these 'little milkmaids' for Poulton Festival, many of whom would become dairy maids. Standing far right at the back is Mary Webster, whose father had a milk round in Staining and Poulton.

Freckleton Holy Trinity School, near Lytham, *c.* 1902. The Domesday Survey refers to the arable soil of Freckleton. When the village became a small port, a mill was built to make sailcloth and sacking. It is believed that the Romans may have landed here.

The double-headed eagle at Rufford Hall, 1962. This is a sure sign of the Fleetwood and Hesketh families, who had such influence in this part of Lancashire. Like the wheat sheaf, it was part of their crest. Situated near Martin Mere, the village of Rufford belonged to the Heskeths, who improved agriculture by draining the mosslands. The half-timbered house was built by Sir Thomas Hesketh early in the fifteenth century, its Great Hall complete with a fine, movable Tudor screen and furniture of the same period. Some twenty years ago the outbuildings housed the crested coach in which Sir Peter Hesketh Fleetwood crossed the Alps in 1834, and which was also used by his uncle, Bold Fleetwood Hesketh. Rufford still holds an annual medieval fair.

Ellen Wright of Marshside near Southport, *c.* 1888. Ellen came from a family who for generations were fishermen. Net braiding, that is making and mending the nets, was part of the women's work. As the tides at Southport receded in the 1840s and Sir Peter Hesketh Fleetwood was inviting fishermen to settle at his new town of Fleetwood, the Wrights, moving their household goods by sea and wagon, came to Fleetwood-on-Wyre and began a new life in Lower Dock Street. Indeed, the Wrights, Leadbetters and Rimmers, all from Marshside, became the mainstay of Fleetwood's inshore fishing industry in the 1890s. Ellen, daughter of Richard Wright, became Mrs Abram, mother of four sons, all of whom were fishermen.

Southport, 1897. The pier, running nearly a mile out to sea, was one of the longest around the coasts of Britain. Since 1863 there had been a Pier Train, the line being electrified in 1905. The train was replaced when the corporation took over its running in 1936. Although the sea was retreating, Southport dubbed itself 'the Montpelier of the North'. Paddling and boating were popular. 'There was entertainment for all tastes; the tumult of a busy day would often end with a firework display' read a 1900 report. In 1875, Prof. Osbourne's high dive from the end of the pier drew crowds, encouraging another 'Professor', Bert Powsey, to do likewise. Queen Victoria's Jubilees were celebrated in similar exuberant fashion, bringing crowds from Liverpool. Among the many wrecks off Southport was that of the *Mexico* in 1886, which cost the lives of two lifeboat crews and was declared a national tragedy. William Bibby of Southport was a lifeboatman of whom it was written: 'He rescued 400 persons from a watery grave.'

Lord Street, Southport, looking east, 1897. The tram is bound for Roe Lane, at a time when crossing streets held little danger. On 5 July 1825, by Act of Parliament, Peter Hesketh and Henry Bold Hoghton, in an exchange of land, provided for the making of Lord Street 88 yards wide.

The Llewelyn Miniature Railway, Southport, early 1900s. This was one of many attractions at this time. The hurdy-gurdy man, hobby horses, water chute, airships and aerial railway were part of a fairground opened in 1903. Besides exploring the river caves, for 3d. you could ride on the Figure 8 Toboggan Railway.

Lytham Pier, 1956. Dr Poole, a resident of the town, described the pier in 1909 as 'centre of the promenaders' joy with a splendid pavilion in the midst of the waves'. Drama, light opera and musical comedy performances were held regularly, and at midsummer one of the best musical festivals in the north of England was held, attracting top performers. In 1928 the pier was almost entirely destroyed by fire – the fate of many a seaside pier. It became an eyesore and locals campaigned for the removal of its rusting structure. After a 9 hour public enquiry the decision was approved, and the pier was demolished in 1960. The opening of Lytham Pier had been one of the town's great days. Easter Monday 1865 saw special trains arriving from Preston with crowds of visitors. The Friendly Societies congregated in Market Place and headed for the new pier, led by the band of the 3rd Lancashire Militia. The Lytham Volunteers formed a guard of honour for the squire's wife, Mrs Eleanor Cecily Clifton, as she came from the Assembly Rooms for the ceremony.

Ashton Gardens, St Anne's-on-Sea, 1918. St George's Gardens were made in 1875 and renamed Ashton Gardens in 1920 as Lord Ashton contributed generously. Mr Porritt and a group of Rossendale businessmen planned the 'Garden City' of St Anne's around these gardens.

The first Ladies' Golf Championship, St Anne's, May 1893. The winner was Lady Margaret Scott (back row, second from right). Today's Royal Lytham and St Anne's Golf Club attracts players and visitors from abroad.

The North Pier, Blackpool, 1895. This is possibly the most famous pier in the world. In the 1900s a postcard from Palestine, addressed simply 'The North Pier', arrived safely. When the first pile was screwed into the clay on 27 June 1862, Maj. Francis Preston, chairman of the North Pier Company, prophesied that Blackpool would 'grow into one of the most amazing aggregations of public amusement in the world'. On 21 May of the following year he formally opened the 1,405 ft long iron structure into which had gone 12,000 tons of metal. For such a red-letter day the townspeople brought back the town crier to greet trippers pouring out of Lancashire and Yorkshire Railway trains. Flags and bunting fluttered all over town and some daredevils could not wait to dive off the end of the pier, where aquatics were to become a speciality. In the grand procession that day were Freemasons, Friendly Societies, fishermen, lifeboatmen, bathing-machine attendants and civic dignitaries. The engineers of Brighton Pier had constructed this 'substantial and safe means for visitors to walk over the sea'. The *Illustrated London News* issued a front-page engraving of the gala opening, and within three years, with a jetty completed, *Clifton* and *Queen of the Bay* pleasure steamers were carrying visitors on trips into the Irish Sea.

Excursion train No. 91 arrives in Blackpool Central Station with hundreds of smiling visitors, Wakes Week 1917. This was when the mill towns closed down and there was a general exodus to the seaside, as depicted in John Trafford Clegg's *Rachda (Rochdale) Wakes*.

Blackpool Carnival, 14 June 1924. This was one of the many annual attractions. 'It is lovely here, but crowded. Yours till Niagara Falls,' wrote Isabel on the back of this postcard.

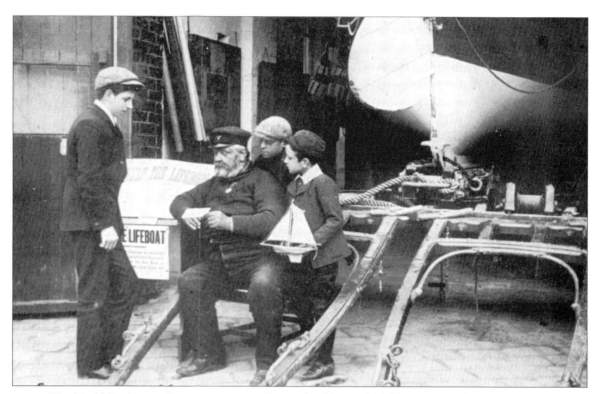

'Owd Jack' Stanhope, a former coxswain, talking to local boys. The lifeboat, mounted on a cart, had to be towed out by strong horses prior to launching. The chairman of the Blackpool Branch of the Royal National Lifeboat Institution was then Robert ('Bob') Bickerstaffe, and the honorary secretary was Mr C.H. Turver, who lived at 40 Market Street. 'Owd Jack', like the chairman Mr Bickerstaffe, was a familiar figure on the seafront. Bob was the lifeboat coxswain for many years as well as central pier manager. Of many rescues by the Blackpool lifeboat, one occurred soon after the opening of the New Promenade in 1870. The *Sprightly* of Preston, bound for Barrow-in-Furness with a load of stone, got into difficulties in a south-westerly gale. The crew of two let down the anchor and hoisted a flag of distress. They were rescued by the *Robert William* lifeboat under coxswain William Parr. This postcard was issued by the Blackpool Branch of the Royal National Lifeboat Institution and posed by Mr Wolstenholme of Wellington Studios, Blackpool.

Great Marton windmill, near Blackpool, restored in 1987. In the eighteenth century, visitors to Blackpool by stagecoach would have seen the mill as they approached. William Hutton, travelling from Birmingham, spoke of good roads but complained of a lack of milestones, so that travellers between Preston and Blackpool were charged for an excess of 2 miles. In the early 1740s the miller William Willans received £12 a year but had to supply all the candles. This tower mill had four storeys, a cellar and a tiny underground passage to the storeroom. Repairs between 1986 and 1987 cost £90,000, when new sails and an improved cap had to be put in place. The original brick was laid bare and weather-resistant paint applied to make the mill gleaming white. Originally it would have been limewashed. The Oxford Hotel or Half Way House was built next to the Great Marton windmill in the late nineteenth century.

Air Raid Precautions (ARP) demonstration, Bispham Cliffs, 1938. The Second World War did not begin until a year later, but, following the Munich crisis, Lancashire towns and cities were on the alert. In the 1930s the high cliffs at Bispham were served by a lift opposite Knowle Avenue, which in later years fell into disrepair. Visitors could be taken down to the boating pool. Bispham's sea defences were repaired with help from the European Community, the last stretch between Duchess Drive and Cavendish Road being completed in late 1989. Coastal erosion had been a constant problem prior to 1905 when Tom Gallon Lumb of Red Bank Road and David Abercrombie, with other local developers, gave evidence at the Shingle Enquiry, Blackpool.

Thornton Hall, Wyre Road, Thornton-le-Fylde. This house belonged to Mr Silcock until the 1930s. He had a Friesian herd of dairy cattle famous throughout the Fylde and also owned a shooting box in Bleasdale, purchased from the Garnett family of Lark Hill, Salford.

Marsh Mill, Thornton Cleveleys, 1936. This mill was built in 1794 by Ralph Slater, millwright, who also built the mills at Pilling and Clifton. For generations, flour was ground here, but when fine white flour was in demand the mill could not cope, so turned instead to grinding animal feed. Owned originally by Bold Fleetwood Hesketh, it is now the centre of a shopping complex.

Woodbine Cottage, Cleveleys, 1901. This thatched, cruck-built dwelling was where John Bright (born 1811), the English statesman who championed free trade, stayed when touring the Fylde. A garage now occupies the site on Victoria Road.

The Belgian trawler *Commandant Bultinck*, which was wrecked at Rossall on 2 October 1929. Boys and masters from Rossall School assisted in the rescue, but two crew members were drowned when they jumped into the sea. They are buried in Fleetwood cemetery.

Fleetwood Dock, 1911. A grain ship is on the right. A deputation of important visitors concerned with the future of the fishing industry had assembled to discuss the extension and modernizing of the dock. In the centre, bowler-hatted and wearing a velvet-collared overcoat, is Cllr James Robertson, with members of the Fleetwood Fishing Vessel Owners' Association, which was formed in 1907. Fleetwood commenced as a port with its own Customs in 1839, and by the following year the first wharf was near completion. Only when tides were favourable could cargoes be unloaded from ships lying at anchor, but the 600 foot iron wharf north of the stone quay enabled ships to tie up alongside. In 1877 the new dock was built and the grain elevator was ready for use. A very busy period for cargo trade ensued with ships coming and going from all parts of the world. Schooners, barques, sloops, full-rigged ships and brigantines brought grain, timber, iron ore, Indian corn, oranges, esparto and china clay. However, trade lapsed with the coming of the Manchester Ship Canal and new designs in ships, which meant that the entrance to Fleetwood Dock was too narrow. The renovation of the dock and concentration on fishing vessels brought in £1.5 million in 1919. In 1911, relations with Iceland were friendly, and this group was unaware of the Cod Wars which were to squeeze the life out of the fishing port.

Fleetwood Pier. The pier went up in flames on 20 August 1952, causing £40,000 worth of damage. It was the biggest fire in the history of the town – worse than the timber fire on the dock or the burning of Wyre Light. Flames could be seen for 20 miles from 10.30 a.m. until midnight. Eight fire engines attended.

Laying of the foundation stone, Methodist chapel, Friday 1 February 1899. This new Methodist chapel was in North Church Street. The opening fund-raiser had been a successful bazaar. Here ladies of the church have gathered to add to the building the bricks that they had been encouraged to buy.

HMS *Fleetwood*, F 47, entering Fleetwood
Dock, May 1937. As the sloop slowly
manouevred, the narrow entrance caused it to
strike the Cornish granite sides of the dock.
Large crowds waved handkerchiefs and
greetings were signalled to the crew from the
top of the Mount. Officers and men were
given the freedom of the town and each day an
average of 8,000 people came to look round
the ship. The Fleetwood Fishing Vessel
Owners' Association entertained Commander
A.C. Chapman and officers to dinner and
presented a silver cup. This was all in honour
of King George VI's Coronation. Fleetwood
trawlers attended a review at Spithead in the
same year.

Arrival of the *Manxman*, Heysham harbour, 1910. The Isle of Man Steam Packet Company was
inaugurated in July 1832. The first steamer, launched on 30 June 1830, was named *Mona's Isle* because
prior to July 1832 the company had been known as the Mona's Isle Company.

Morecambe's busy promenade, Summer 1909. Note the rare, newfangled motor car among the landaus. The loaded tram is heading for the popular Winter Gardens. Morecambe's pier was destroyed in the 1977 storm.

Winter Gardens and Promenade, Morecambe. This reveals the grandeur of Morecambe's chief attraction, which offered dancing, theatrical turns, a café, restaurant and billiards, all in splendid surroundings. The view across Morecambe Bay to the fells of the Lake District was unrivalled.

Bare village, *c*. 1918. This developed as an extension of Morecambe seaside resort, until by 1930 Morecambe Promenade stretched all the way to Bare with its popular bathing pool and hotels for visitors.

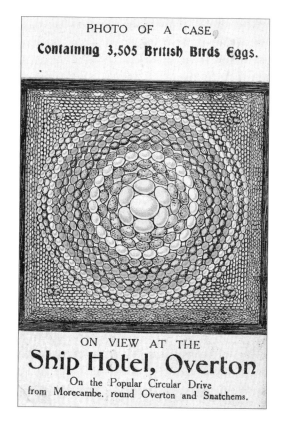

Advertisement for the Ship Hotel, Overton. Early this century the Ship Hotel had a case containing 3,505 British birds' eggs, which attracted visitors on the popular Circular Drive from Morecambe to Overton and Snatchems.

Devil's Bridge (the farther of the two), the River Lune, Kirkby Lonsdale, 1904. According to legend, the thirteenth-century packhorse bridge was built by the Devil himself. An old lady was distressed because her cow had strayed over the river on to the opposite bank. How was she to get it back? The Devil promised her that he would build a bridge overnight, provided that the first living thing to pass over it became his. She agreed to the bargain and returned the next day with a small dog hidden under her cloak. She flung her cloak, together with meat, on to the bridge. Away dashed the dog towards Old Nick, who had hoped for the old woman's soul. It is said that by looking downstream the Devil's neck collar can be discerned. Not only did he leave finger marks on the coping, but in his fury, the story goes, he dropped stones and boulders: a pile at the head of Kingdale and a cairn on Casterton Fell. Weekly market day in Kirkby Lonsdale is Thursday, and in early September a two-day Victorian Fair is held. A new market square was built in 1822 after the 1820 fire, which destroyed the coaching inn, the Rose and Crown, and killed five women. The new Royal Hotel was where Queen Adelaide stayed. She gave instructions that the red flannel laid out for her to step on should be made into petticoats for the poor women of Kirkby Lonsdale.

Britannia Class locomotive *Solway Firth*, No. 70049, hauls a Glasgow to Manchester express through Carnforth station, August 1961. The railway arrived at Carnforth in 1857. This station was used as the set for the film *Brief Encounter*, starring Trevor Howard.

Cove Lane, Silverdale, 1959. This lane led to the shore, covered with sea pinks. Situated in the garden of a house dated 1816, Lindeth Tower at Silverdale, a battlemented square tower of three storeys was where Mrs Elizabeth Gaskell stayed occasionally.

The Pier, Grange-over-Sands, 1902. At this time, boating was popular, with trips to Holme Island. The resort developed with the arrival of the Furness Railway in 1857. The Netherwood Hotel, originally called Blawith, was built as a private house in 1893.

Kellet village, about 5 miles from Lancaster, September 1913. The village had a population of 284 in 1861. Dunaldmill Hole was a cavern in the limestone rock where a stream turned a small mill-wheel, then disappeared underground to reappear at Carnforth.

Cartmel Priory Church, 1912. Apart from the priory church at Lancaster, this was the only monastic church in Lancashire to escape destruction at the time of the Dissolution. For eighty years the roof was off and windows broken, but George Preston of Holker Hall restored it, thus saving the wonderful oak canopies in the choir stalls.

Craftsman Mr Wall, dry-stone walling in the Furness district of Lancashire, 1963. So practised was Mr Wall that, once he had picked up and placed a stone, he never needed to reposition it.

Holker village, near Cark, 1907. The most famous building here is the Cavendish family home, Holker
Hall, which was rebuilt in 1840 but still has an old wing dating from the seventeenth century. Prince
Philip stayed here when he took his coach and four across Morecambe Bay accompanied by the Sands
guide, Cedric Robinson. The Holker mosslands were famed for 'May' (hawthorn) trees.

Shrimping on the shore, Flookburgh, *c.* 1900. The tools of this trade were rakes, riddles and baskets.
Near Flookburgh is fifteenth-century Wraysholme Pele Tower, which originally had three storeys and was
one of a chain of towers built as a defence against Scottish raiders.

Market Street, Ulverston, 1920. In one corner a building dated 1762 was probably the Market House. In Union Street is the 1845 Savings Bank. Engineer Rennie built a canal from Ulverston to the sea. When it silted up, Barrow became the main harbour.

Greenodd Station, 1904. Greenodd was once a flourishing iron-ore port with a shipbuilding community. At one time Furness ports exported 75,000 tons of iron ore per year, miners being paid 1s. a day. Both Greenodd and Ulverston were creeks under Lancaster.

Penny Bridge and Hall, 1900. A small landing place like Spark Bridge, it became unusable because of silting. Liverpool slaveship masters used to leave black men at Penny Bridge to be collected by the agent from Storrs Hall, Windermere, whose owner was known as the poet William Wordsworth.

Lady of the Lake afloat on Lake Windermere at Newby Bridge, last century. This craft was built at Greenodd by Richard Ashburner. *Lord of the Isles* lies beached. Near the eighteenth-century Swan Hotel with its columned doorway, the five-arched bridge was built of slate in the 1600s.

Duke Street, Barrow-in-Furness, early 1900s. Rayner's hosier and hatters is on the right. Locomotive superintendent James Ramsden became the first mayor in 1867, the year in which the railway company built Devonshire Dock.

The launch of a Vickers Naval airship, Barrow, early this century. In 1840, when Ulverston's population was 5,000, Barrow's was only 300, but H.W. Schneider opened up the area after discovery of the Park deposit of iron. The chief landowners were the Dukes of Devonshire and Buccleugh.

Walney Ferry, Barrow-in-Furness, 3 August 1906. This ferry was indispensable for cyclists, ponies and traps, basket-laden errand boys and passengers. In 1908 it was replaced by a bridge. Walney had a lighthouse built on its stormy tip in 1799, but *Angelique* was wrecked there in a great gale on 23 January 1836.

The bridge at Walney, 1915. Vickerstown was built on Walney Island, aiming at the ideals of Port Sunlight, to house Barrow shipyard workers as there was insufficient accommodation on the mainland. Commenced in 1901, by 1904 there were 930 houses available.

Charcoal burning near Broughton-in-Furness, 1920. Charcoal was made by piling wood into pyramids, covering the pile with earth and leaving it to smoulder. It was a slow, skilled process used by the workmen who lived in huts in the forest, occasionally visited by their families. It was used at Backbarrow and at the Low Wood Gunpowder factory. In the thirteenth century the monks of Furness Abbey used charcoal for smelting iron ore.

The Friends' Meeting House, Colthouse near Hawkshead, *c.* 1930. For their settlements the Quakers sought out remote valleys and heights to avoid persecution. William Wordsworth lodged for a time in the hamlet when he attended Hawkshead Grammar School.

Coniston station, 1957. Engine No. 41217 with a push-and-pull train is waiting under wrought-iron bridge No. 30. In 1900 an Anglo-Saxon cross was placed in St Andrew's Church as a monument to the great Victorian John Ruskin who lived at Brantwood, overlooking Coniston Water.

The gondola on Coniston Water, 1882. Coniston Water was one of the most beautiful parts of Lancashire, but has now been lost to Cumbria. Launched on Coniston in 1859, the gondola served until 1937, then was abandoned for forty years until National Trust staff restored it to ply once more, carrying eighty-six passengers.

Packhorse bridge, Rusland, near Finsthwaite, towards the end of the nineteenth century. This tranquil scene is a photograph taken by pioneer photographer Alfred Pettit, who was established in the Lake District as early as 1860. Although less well known than the Abraham brothers, he was the original purveyor of 'sun pictures', as early photographs were termed simply because the prints were made by exposing them in sunlight. Alfred and his daughter Lucie were, first and foremost, skilled painters, and their work was on display in the handsome building on St John's Street, Keswick, an art gallery owned and run by Pettit. Because visitors wanted souvenirs of this beautiful and newly discovered area, he turned to photography to supply mementoes. At that time the Abrahams, Maysons and the father of Beatrix Potter were all achieving good results. Alfred installed his photographic studio in the gallery and concentrated on skilful interpretation of light and shade, using 'all the mysterious paraphernalia for catching and committing indelibly to paper the true life reflections of the human image and the most interesting views of the district'. Two years before his death, Pettit, who portrayed peace and solitude in his photography, painted a set of pictures that were purchased by Manchester Corporation for the State Room of their new Town Hall.

ACKNOWLEDGEMENTS

For the use of old postcards and illustrations my special thanks are due to Preston's 'Mr Toop', Cliff Hayes of Northern Publishing Services and Gordon Coltas of Locofotos. I should also like to acknowledge the help of Aurora Publications; Elsie Ayrton; Blackpool Branch of the RNLI; Edna Brown; Mrs K. Brown; Stanley Butterworth; Laura Clark; the *Garstang Courier*; Dorothy and Jim Hince; Lancashire Federation of Women's Institutes; Lilywhite Ltd (Brighouse); Lytham St Anne's Library; Merseyside County Museum; Eric Mills; Harold Monks; Tony Nickson; Susan Orchard; Department of Chemistry, University of Lancaster; and Hazel Walker.

INDEX

BRITAIN IN OLD PHOTOGRAPHS

Lincoln
Lincoln Cathedral
The Lincolnshire Coast
Liverpool
Around Llandudno
Around Lochaber
Theatrical London
Around Louth
The Lower Fal Estuary
Lowestoft
Luton
Lympne Airfield
Lytham St Annes
Maidenhead
Around Maidenhead
Around Malvern
Manchester
Manchester Road & Rail
Mansfield
Marlborough: A Second Selection
Marylebone & Paddington
Around Matlock
Melton Mowbray
Around Melksham
The Mendips
Merton & Morden
Middlesbrough
Midsomer Norton & Radstock
Around Mildenhall
Milton Keynes
Minehead
Monmouth & the River Wye
The Nadder Valley
Newark
Around Newark
Newbury
Newport, Isle of Wight
The Norfolk Broads
Norfolk at War
North Fylde
North Lambeth
North Walsham & District
Northallerton
Northampton
Around Norwich
Nottingham 1944–74
The Changing Face of Nottingham
Victorian Nottingham
Nottingham Yesterday & Today
Nuneaton
Around Oakham
Ormskirk & District
Otley & District
Oxford: The University
Oxford Yesterday & Today
Oxfordshire Railways: A Second
   Selection
Oxfordshire at School
Around Padstow
Pattingham & Wombourne

Penwith
Penzance & Newlyn
Around Pershore
Around Plymouth
Poole
Portsmouth
Poulton-le-Fylde
Preston
Prestwich
Pudsey
Radcliffe
RAF Chivenor
RAF Cosford
RAF Hawkinge
RAF Manston
RAF Manston: A Second Selection
RAF St Mawgan
RAF Tangmere
Ramsgate & Thanet Life
Reading
Reading: A Second Selection
Redditch & the Needle District
Redditch: A Second Selection
Richmond, Surrey
Rickmansworth
Around Ripley
The River Soar
Romney Marsh
Romney Marsh: A Second
   Selection
Rossendale
Around Rotherham
Rugby
Around Rugeley
Ruislip
Around Ryde
St Albans
St Andrews
Salford
Salisbury
Salisbury: A Second Selection
Salisbury: A Third Selection
Around Salisbury
Sandhurst & Crowthorne
Sandown & Shanklin
Sandwich
Scarborough
Scunthorpe
Seaton, Lyme Regis & Axminster
Around Seaton & Sidmouth
Sedgley & District
The Severn Vale
Sherwood Forest
Shrewsbury
Shrewsbury: A Second Selection
Shropshire Railways
Skegness
Around Skegness
Skipton & the Dales
Around Slough

Smethwick
Somerton & Langport
Southampton
Southend-on-Sea
Southport
Southwark
Southwell
Southwold to Aldeburgh
Stafford
Around Stafford
Staffordshire Railways
Around Staveley
Stepney
Stevenage
The History of Stilton Cheese
Stoke-on-Trent
Stoke Newington
Stonehouse to Painswick
Around Stony Stratford
Around Stony Stratford: A Second
   Selection
Stowmarket
Streatham
Stroud & the Five Valleys
Stroud & the Five Valleys: A
   Second Selection
Stroud's Golden Valley
The Stroudwater and Thames &
   Severn Canals
The Stroudwater and Thames &
   Severn Canals: A Second
   Selection
Suffolk at Work
Suffolk at Work: A Second
   Selection
The Heart of Suffolk
Sunderland
Sutton
Swansea
Swindon: A Third Selection
Swindon: A Fifth Selection
Around Tamworth
Taunton
Around Taunton
Teesdale
Teesdale: A Second Selection
Tenbury Wells
Around Tettenhall & Codshall
Tewkesbury & the Vale of
   Gloucester
Thame to Watlington
Around Thatcham
Around Thirsk
Thornbury to Berkeley
Tipton
Around Tonbridge
Trowbridge
Around Truro
TT Races
Tunbridge Wells

Tunbridge Wells: A Second
   Selection
Twickenham
Uley, Dursley & Cam
The Upper Fal
The Upper Tywi Valley
Uxbridge, Hillingdon & Cowley
The Vale of Belvoir
The Vale of Conway
Ventnor
Wakefield
Wallingford
Walsall
Waltham Abbey
Wandsworth at War
Wantage, Faringdon & the Vale
   Villages
Around Warwick
Weardale
Weardale: A Second Selection
Wednesbury
Wells
Welshpool
West Bromwich
West Wight
Weston-super-Mare
Around Weston-super-Mare
Weymouth & Portland
Around Wheatley
Around Whetstone
Whitchurch to Market Drayton
Around Whitstable
Wigton & the Solway Plain
Willesden
Around Wilton
Wimbledon
Around Windsor
Wingham, Addisham &
   Littlebourne
Wisbech
Witham & District
Witney
Around Witney
The Witney District
Wokingham
Around Woodbridge
Around Woodstock
Woolwich
Woolwich Royal Arsenal
Around Wootton Bassett,
   Cricklade & Purton
Worcester
Worcester in a Day
Around Worcester
Worcestershire at Work
Around Worthing
Wotton-under-Edge to Chipping
   Sodbury
Wymondham & Attleborough
The Yorkshire Wolds

To order any of these titles please telephone our distributor, Littlehampton Book Services on 01903 721596
For a catalogue of these and our other titles please ring Regina Schinner on 01453 731114